Decks

BY WALTER IAN FISCHMAN

GROSSET
GOOD LIFE
BOOKS

PUBLISHERS • GROSSET & DUNLAP • NEW YORK

Acknowledgments

Cover photograph by Mort Engel

The author wishes to express his appreciation to the following for their permission to use the drawings and photographs in this book: Morley Baer, photographer, p. 24 top left; California Redwood Association: p. 8 top, p. 16 top, p.18 top, p. 18 bottom, p. 20, p. 26 top left, p. 26 bottom left, p. 32 top right, p. 34 top left, p. 34 right, p. 60 bottom, p. 70 top, p. 70 bottom, p. 71 top right, p. 87 bottom; Campbell & Wong, architects, p. 24 top left; Anthony Tallarico: p. 14, p. 15 top, p. 42 top, p. 43 middle left, p. 47, p. 48, p. 49, p. 50, p. 51, p. 52, p. 53, p. 59 top left, p. 59 middle left, p. 59 top right, p. 61 bottom; Erecto-Pat, Inc.: p. 56, p. 57, p. 60 top, p. 61 top, p. 62, p. 77, p. 78 top left, p. 78 top right, p. 79 top left, p. 79 bottom left; Hort-Pix: p. 5, p. 6 bottom, p. 7 bottom, p. 11, p. 15 bottom, p. 16 bottom, p. 22 top left, p. 22 bottom left, p. 23 top, p. 23 bottom, p. 24 bottom left, p. 24 bottom right, p. 25 top, p. 25 bottom, p. 27 top right, p. 27 bottom, p. 30 left, p. 32 left, p. 32 bottom right, p. 38, p. 59 bottom, p. 66, p. 68 top, p. 68 bottom, p. 69 right, p. 71 bottom right, p. 72, p. 73, p. 74, p. 76, p. 78 bottom, p. 79 right, p. 86, p. 88, p. 93, p. 94; Elvin McDonald: p. 12, p. 24 top right, p. 29 bottom, p. 31, p. 34 bottom left, p. 44 top, p. 44 bottom, p. 87 top, p. 91; Don Reiman, architect, p. 33 top, p. 33 bottom; Teco: p. 42 bottom, p. 43 top right, p. 43 top left, p. 43 bottom left, p. 43 right, p. 45, p. 68 right, p. 69 left, p. 70 bottom right, p. 71 bottom left; Western Wood Products Association: p. 4, p. 6 top, p. 7 top, p. 8 bottom, p. 9, p. 21, p. 22 right, p. 24 top left, p. 26 top right, p. 27 top left, p. 28, p. 29 top, p. 30 top right, p. 30 bottom right, p. 36, p. 37, p. 64, p. 65, p. 80, p. 81, p. 82, p. 83, p. 84.

Instructions and safety precautions in this book have been carefully checked for accuracy. However, the author and publisher do not warrant or guarantee results and cannot be responsible for any adverse consequences resulting from the use of information contained herein. The author has attempted to assist the reader in avoiding problems by setting forth appropriate and recommended procedures.

Contents

1
Decks, Terraces, and Patios

If you'd like to add a fantastic amount of living space to your existing home and do it easily and inexpensively, here's happy news for you: a deck, a terrace, or a patio may very well be the ideal answer to that cramped feeling that's been pervading the homestead. But, before you make the investment of time and money, you will have to review some of your attitudes to make sure they are in step with today's concepts of outdoor living.

First, are you an extreme case of an Indoor Person? Do you feel comfortable entertaining your friends only at a formally set dining table? Do you dislike sunlight, or do you find it difficult to breathe fresh air?

If you answered "yes" to these questions, a deck, patio, or terrace may not be for you.

A sunny pebbled patio bordering a pool shaded on the far side.

Left: A sunny morning spot off the living room, where you can take your coffee, is separate from an adjoining deck off the bedroom, where the morning and evening view can start and end the day.

The greatest asset of a deck is that it extends a large level area from the house, regardless of the uneven terrain below. Not every deck needs the sleek bench that acts as a railing here, but it adds distinction to the simple deck and concrete steps.

Here a flagstone terrace proved too limited for outdoor living. With the ground falling rapidly into a ravine, a deck proved the perfect answer, offering more room for dining and lounging beneath the large dramatic limbs of an old ash tree rising through openings in the deck.

But, if you sometimes wish you could entertain guests casually, or if you feel you miss seeing sunlight and a bit of nature occasionally, you could probably adapt to outdoor living without great difficulty.

Hidebound tradition has caught most of us in a rut that defines our living space as bounded by four walls and a roof. But many people have found an excitement and a freedom in extending their lives beyond their front, side, or back doors—finding relaxation, sunshine, outdoor cooking, and entertaining in the open air entirely to their liking.

Planning

Properly planned, this open space outside the walls of your present home can give you a living space that's as big, or even twice as big, as what you've already got inside the house—depending upon the space that's available or convenient to use, and depending upon whether you prefer to install a deck, a terrace, or a patio.

By the definition of this book, a patio is an outdoor living surface that is raised up slightly from the ground so that there is a small amount of air space underneath it. This might be six inches to a foot between the ground and the floor space. A deck will be considerably higher—two to six feet off the ground generally, though some decks (such as those extending from a second floor) can be even higher. Also, a patio generally tends to be a smaller surface, while the deck takes in more square footage. A terrace is generally set into the ground and is, for the most part, level with the ground; and it is usually made of stone, brick, or tile, only occasionally made of wood.

Which of these forms would fit in most suitably with the architecture, design, or structure of your house? Which form do you feel you would most enjoy? Which form do you think you could make the best use of? Allow yourself the luxury of dreaming for a moment. Perhaps you would like a quiet corner to sleep in the sun. Perhaps you are tired of parties where your friends step on each other, spill drinks on sofas and chairs, and leave cigarette burns in your carpet.

Considering Your Lifestyle

When you stop to think, the chances are that you may have many wishes, needs, or requirements that could be answered by an outdoor extension to your home. Before you decide on deck, patio, or terrace, decide exactly what purposes it will serve in your private or your social life. Consider the possibilities:

Taking it Easy: When most people consider a deck, terrace, or patio, they generally think of a place to relax and take life easy. You may feel that just any old place will do for this purpose. Not true. Your idea of relaxation may be quite different from that of your next-door neighbor. Since this is going to be *your* space, why not tailor it to *your* kind of loafing?

Do you do your loafing principally in the evening? Or do you have spare time during the day? How about weekends? Do you prefer sunshine or shade? Or do you like to keep both options open? Do you like to take a snooze before dinner—or after dinner? How about the quiet time just before you head for bed, the gentle half hour when you can slowly savor a nightcap and let the cares of the day drift away while you shift gears preparatory to sleep?

Soaking up the Sun: We live in an age of Sun Worship, where looking tanned is synonymous with looking healthy. Some people can tan quickly and easily, and some have to work at it—laboriously. To get a nice even, all-over tan may require a great deal of privacy—finding an open space that is somehow sheltered from view. Some people, with sensitive skin, find that they may fall asleep in the sun and bake too long. Can you plan your deck, patio, or terrace so that you have just the right combination of openness, shelter, or shade to get just the amount of sun you need, with the privacy you need, and with the protection you may require?

Escaping with Hobbies or Recreation: Do you like indoor plants, and would you like to enjoy them outside when warm weather comes? Do you like to putter with repairing household appliances, but get complaints

With roof extended, this built-on deck-bedroom becomes part of the house. There are closets behind the sliding panels of the back wall, half of which serve the living room deck on the other side.

Broad wooden planks surround the concrete skirt of this swimming pool. Wood is cooler to the feet than concrete is, and it is never slippery. Most important of all, the wood and plastic screen surrounding the pool and connecting with the house is here (as in most of the country) required by law.

Egg-crate roof, thin slatted fence, checkerboard deck pattern and simple deck furniture—it all has a very contemporary look.

A practical way of building on—car-port and tool-house beneath a solid deck (not easy to maintain in a waterproof condition except with epoxy, but otherwise carefree).

about messing up the living room or wreaking havoc on the dining-room table? Do you wish you had a recreation room where you could work off excess energy or hostility with a bit of competitive exercise? A deck, patio, or terrace can be built with space for indoor-outdoor gardening shelves, or for worktables, or for a folding tennis table.

Cooking or Dining with Nature: Do you feel your natural foods would taste better if they were cooked and eaten in natural surroundings? Or do you simply feel hampered and hemmed in by the four walls of your kitchen? Have you dreamed of having your morning eggs and coffee surrounded by the morning sun and breeze while keeping the binoculars at hand to spot your neighborhood birds? If your deck, patio, or terrace—or part of it—can be built with easy access to your kitchen, your dreams can be fulfilled.

Entertaining: Are you a gregarious, party-loving individual, but the narrow confines of your living room or dining room seem to be cramping your style? Do your cocktail guests like to spread out in conversational groups? Do you like the informality of buffet dining? Do you wish you had the room so that your guests could dance if they wanted to? Then you'd better plan your deck, patio, or terrace with this in mind. You'll want to ask yourself if you won't want to include some form of roof or awning—or perhaps provision for a bar, or even a hi-fi system.

Getting What You Want: You may want your outdoor living space to serve many purposes. You may not be able to have it serve all these at once, but if you consider carefully, you can have it satisfy those you feel are most important to you.

And, since you're not starting from scratch with house and outdoor living space, you will not have the opportunity to rotate the entire structure into the best position. You have to work with what you have. Take the time to look at the proposed location, observing it from early morning until sunset to see just where and when you have sun and shade. Does it conform to your living schedule? Where are streets, driveways, trees or shrubbery? Will you have interference from street noise? Will existing trees and shrubbery give you needed privacy?

Dream about your Shangri-La, but carefully consider each aspect of your project, and determine how much of it you can make a reality.

Planning the Site

Since it's not very likely that you're going to build a brand new terrace and a brand new house at the same time, your new outdoor living space is an add-on. As a result, from the very beginning, it comes with a set of built-in restrictions. For example, you can't just position it wherever you want. You must take into consideration the existing structure of the house. If there are trees on your lot, these will affect what you do. Driveways, roads, streets, neighbors, fences—all of these affect the design and planning of decks, patios, and terraces.

But don't despair. Just working your way around the existing hassles can result in unusual and exciting solutions. Try to regard existing problems as random opportunity. Since the new expansion is for fun, and since there are quite likely a great many possible solutions, it's highly improbable that you'll make any disastrous blunders. Accept the problems and the planning as another source of pleasure. Most certainly it's the best way to reach a happy solution.

Since this will be your personal addition to the house, your planning should accommodate your own individual needs and requirements. For example, you may prefer a cozy feeling to the patio. That's easy to acquire. It merely hinges on orientation to the space, plus a bit of imagination in incorporating visual and audial barriers. If you live in an area where a sunny nook away from the cutting edge of wind is desirable, the planning solution again is principally one of orientation. Find out the direction of the prevailing winds, and screen off the space by using the house itself or by using a series of windbreaks.

Pay special attention to the idea of utilizing the sun. In your mind, follow through with the accessibility of each of the rooms in

A small house with a standard deck added, an outdoor grill, a tree bench, and bordering benches with slanting backs. A perfect place for relaxing with family and friends.

the house so that you can get a better feeling for the functions you want the outdoor spaces to fulfill.

Existing structures are factors that must be taken into consideration. Your house is number one on the list since it's not very portable. However, large trees, large rocks, driveways, streets, and the like also have a tendency to stay put. For this reason, your new construction must be situated in and around what's already there. Again, your approach to this problem can evoke despair or delight at the prospect of a creative search.

Building Codes

Building codes and building restrictions are a reality of life, but they are far less stringent for an outside structure than for inside. It's important that you familiarize yourself with them at the outset. For example, the regulations may say that you cannot build any closer than a specified number of feet from the property line. While you may be able to get a variance approval from the appropriate group (zoning board or building department), it is more likely that you'll have to adhere to the letter of the law. But you must realize that, viewed in the large picture, this sticky rigidity does make sense. Since the regulations were usually enacted to insure good construction and a kind of harmony for the entire neighborhood, too many exceptions would spoil the area.

Improving Architecture

In the planning stage you have a wonderful opportunity to simplify construction. There are many aspects of building that are quite difficult and possibly expensive. By merely bypassing these, you can make the job easier. For example, if at all possible, avoid the following nifties:

The Hazardous "Waterproof" Deck: Most of the decks in this book have been designed to let rainwater and snow sift through to the ground below. The flooring is deliberately planned with gaps between the boards. If you are to transform this open grillwork into a completely waterproof surface, you'll have to lock yourself into a complicated type of construction. In effect, you'll have to build a roof that you can walk on. Since you want the surface to be level and flat, the hassle gets even more involved because the snow and the rain will accumulate on the surface.

Of course, there's an easy way around all of this: don't do it. Follow the advice given in the following pages. Plan your deck with open construction so that water and snow can pass through.

Adjusting the House to Fit the Deck: Avoid the temptation to pick out a site that requires extensive structural changes in the house itself in order to accommodate the addition. For example, if you are carried away by enthusiasm, it's easy to commit the error of deciding "what an ideal spot this would be, if only we had a door here." Depending upon the type of exterior walls you have, adding a door can range all the way from being merely expensive, difficult, and time-consuming to a devastating experience, such as weakening the structure of the wall.

You can, however, convert a window into a doorway, depending on the type of siding you have on your home. A wood-sheathed house demands the least amount of demolition and new construction; it's the easiest to tackle. Brick or stone siding gets into the realm of major construction.

"It's the Only Space I've Got": One homeowner built a patio in the only available space —right in the front of the house. Unhappily the street on which the house faced was a very busy one with a great deal of traffic and noise. After considering all possibilities, the homeowner built a mound garden of earth, as close as possible to the property line in front. This bulwark was about four feet tall and was planted in groundcover and scattered with found stones and rock-garden plants. The effect was quite handsome from both sides. But more important, just that bit of dirt with its crown of plants blocked off nearly 75 percent of the annoying sounds coming from the street. The engine racket, the horns,

the screeching brakes, still sounded, but were now muffled—not nearly so insistent and far less intrusive.

For some people, sound is the big element of privacy. Unfortunately this is difficult to achieve. However, dense planting will help. So will orientation of the space away from the source of sound. Although the whole question of sound intrusion can never be totally licked, there are effective remedies for almost every hassle. Just don't look for 100 percent control of this problem.

The Romantic Cantilever and Other Special Problems: Unless you have the services of a professional architect or engineer, don't consider the idea of cantilevering a deck out from the side of your house. Beautiful? Sure, it can be quite beautiful. It makes for a nice clean line, free of obvious supports so that the deck appears to float in space. However, the construction problems involved are enough to gray the hair of the well-intended amateur.

Concepts like this are delightful in the abstract sense. But do not, without solid professional assistance, try to tackle this or any other far-out design concept by yourself.

By the same token, seek out professional guidance if you absolutely insist on having the deck built out over water, a marsh, a sandy beach, or any other ground that's not completely solid. There are special problems involved in construction of this nature. Sure they can be solved. But the know-how is not within average ken. Furthermore, even if you call in a professional carpenter to handle this phase of the work, you won't be able to hire just any artisan at all. Unless he has had a great deal of experience and a proven track record in successfully completing this type of construction, you can still run into trouble. Generally, while the final effect of a cantilevered deck can be handsome indeed, the mechanical hazards and uncertainties can sometimes verge on the tragic.

A mound garden alongside the roadway buffers the traffic noise from the large deck and pool beyond.

2
Create Your Own Climate-by Plan

While there are advantages and disadvantages to all of the possible exposures for your new outdoor living area, you will probably not have a free hand. Existing conditions and structures tend to lock you into situations of limited choice. However, if you do have any maneuvering room, here briefly are the advantages and disadvantages of various exposures.

North: If you're building in a hot climate or a locale that is exposed to intense sunlight, building on the northern exposure can cut down on the searing heat. If the living area extends away from the house to any extent at all, you can wind up with a nice combination of sun and shade. A single story house will (except for high noon) give a ribbon of shadow ranging from a narrow band to a sizable swath across the surface. On the other hand, a two-story house can extend the shadow area considerably further, and this might not be an entirely happy situation.

East: This orientation is better for a warm climate than for a cold one. This exposure gets mostly morning action. From noontime on, you can probably find a sheltered, shady spot away from the direct rays of the sun if that's what you want. Late afternoons, however, can be chilly, except in midsummer.

West: Hot afternoon midsummer sun will streak in on a deck with a western exposure. If this tends to be excessive, you may need sun louvers or some other form of shade. Summer, early fall, some spring days, and the milder part of winter make up an extended season when you can use a deck, patio, or terrace with this exposure.

South: An area with this orientation tends to get sun in all seasons, if not partially shaded. This means you should be able to use it a good portion of the entire year. All that warmth can be a mixed blessing, however, since it extends from the low-slanting winter rays right through to the midsummer overhead blast. Build an overhang, or grow vines.

Beyond these compass points, terraces that combine geographical orientation such as northeast, southeast, southwest, merely combine the virtues and drawbacks of the two directions that are in their makeup. For your calculations, just figure a mid-point blending of the various qualities.

Left: How to get what you want when you want it. A western-facing sunbathing deck with wind baffles on both sides, combined with an informal shady outdoor dining nook for morning or evening.

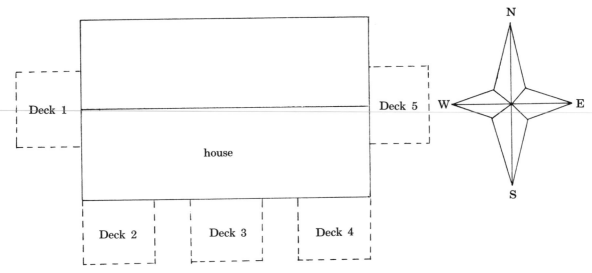

Sun exposure to determine desired position of deck. Decks with south and southwest exposure are warmest in winter, without shade.

Deck 1 West: hot summer exposure, afternoon, if not shaded. Shaded by house during day.

Deck 2 Southwest: hottest summer exposure, afternoon, if not shaded. No house shade summer or winter.

Deck 3 South: hot summer exposure, afternoon, if not shaded. No house shade summer or winter.

Deck 4 Southeast: cool summer exposure, morning, if not shaded. No house shade summer or winter.

Deck 5 East: cool summer exposure, morning only. Shaded by house rest of day.

At the latitude of New York, a 2½-foot overhang will shade a one-story glass wall of house in summer. In winter, sun will penetrate glass wall 25 feet into house. At other latitudes, shade of overhang during summer can be determined by holding up a broad stick at first- or second-story level to determine best overhang for summer shade.

Put It on Paper

Once you've assembled your various ideas, talked over the project thoroughly, reviewed your cigar-box full of clippings (all those ideas that sounded so great when you read about them in magazines) you're probably ready to start making some sort of rough sketch.

Don't panic. There's no need for artistic drawing ability. Get a ruler and a tape measure. At the stationery store, pick up a pad of large graph paper. Be sure to get the type that has large squares to represent a foot, so you'll be able to make a proportional sketch on a scale of 1 square to equal 1 foot. That means that 6 feet would then be represented by 6 squares, and so forth. It makes the whole thing easier to calculate.

Go outdoors with the long tape measure and a helper. Measure the existing area, including the house, driveway, sidewalk, fences, and any other structures. Figure out the ones that will be in direct contact with the new deck, such as trees and large boulders or rock ledges, and transfer them onto the graph paper. Don't try to make all the measurements at one time and then block in the areas on the grid. Instead, transfer the dimensions as you go.

Once you've made a careful compilation of what's already there, it's time to figure what you want to add, how much, and where. The most difficult part of this job for a good many people is the space. It's difficult to keep it straight in your head and only a little easier to work with in a sketch.

To obtain a full realization of the physical areas that you're working with, stop now and then to mark out the areas in full size. For example, if you're sketching out a terrace, step outdoors with a ball of white string. Measure out the size and shape right on the ground. Step back and take a careful look. If you're going to incorporate such features as a dining area, put a table and chairs where your outside furniture will be and see how they can fit. You'd be surprised at how your concepts can change with this procedure.

You can achieve a similar view by constructing a model. Pick up some small sheets of styrofoam at the dime store. This is usually sold in the department with the gift wrappings or the garden supplies. Or you may buy the material in a craft or hobby supply store. Using the foam, cut out little shapes to represent chairs, tables, benches, floormats, and other furnishings that you will want in your outdoor living area. Make these in scale too. Simply measure a bench or lounge chair or plan the charcoal grill you want. If it turns out to be 6 feet long, then the plastic model should be 6 squares long. This will give you a better feeling for the space than trying to play it by eye.

Gradually through this combination of actual measurement plus scale representation, you'll be able to evolve a pretty good concept of what your new outdoor space should look like. But don't despair if it changes a bit when the project actually gets underway. This is par for the course, and if anything, the watchword should be "stay flexible."

Professional Help at Hand

In case the idea of tackling this enormous job on your own seems terrifying, you can hedge your bet by employing professionals. Their assistance can range all the way from taking over the complete job from start-to-finish to a part-time situation where they lend some assistance where needed. In addition there are several possible working relationships midway between these two.

Professional Part-Time: Some homeowners find that it has worked out quite well when they called in professional assistance to tackle certain phases of the work. Generally

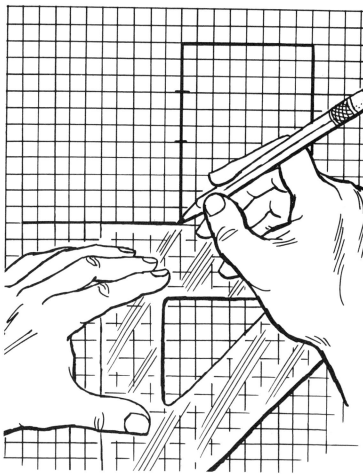

Planning of deck on graph paper.

In the bright sea sun, a wide shielding cedar roof, with plastic panels for light, protects a solid floor.

A rooftop deck, simple, shaded with a wood and plastic roof against the noonday sun (but sunny in winter), and with screened railings. Just off the main bedroom, it accommodates rugged guests or plenty of teenagers in sleeping bags (cots provided).

An expansive suburban backyard lot, for dining and for sit-down gardening along the broad plank borders, and with a lawn for strolling around the borders of flowers and shrubs.

this includes such aspects as digging and pouring foundation pillars, putting up the underpinnings of the new structure, assembling the structural supports, and so forth. Depending on your own competence and abilities, this can be a very workable middle course. For example, you may not be pleased at all with the digging for concrete foundation posts or laying a concrete slab for a terrace. Fine. Call in a professional with full equipment for this. Then you can take over the job of spreading the crushed rock or gravel and putting down the new, attractive surface.

Similarly, many people feel that working with concrete is a rough, nasty job. You can avoid the bother by utilizing other professional services available via the yellow pages of your phone book, or friends who know a reliable person whose work you can see. The determination is strictly your own. You are the only one who really knows how much you can tackle. However, don't be discouraged at the outset. At least try each job. If it's too much for you, you'll realize it quickly enough. On the other hand, there's an equally good chance that you might discover competence you never knew you had.

Contractor/Builder: Before you call in someone to take on the entire job, there's another kind of relationship you might consider. In many areas of the country, it's sometimes possible to get a stonemason or carpenter who will let you act as his assistant instead of bringing in his own. There's a great deal more involved than fetching the tools out of the truck. He will expect you to take over routine tasks under his direction. The big advantage in this procedure is that he is there on the spot to fend problems. The panic rate drops considerably under this situation. Here again the evaluation will have to be your own. If you have a reasonable competence with tools, if you can drive a nail without battering the work and if you can saw a respectably straight line, you're probably sufficiently equipped to tackle the job of a carpenter's assistant. Let the professional figure out what to do and direct your work.

In the same way, you may not be able to lay bricks, but there's no reason why you can't mix mortar and lug it to the spot where the professional mason is working. Even simple manual labor can speed the work considerably. If the mason doesn't have to bring in the bricks as he needs them, but is always assured of a supply stacked right at hand, if there's someone to hold the other end of the ladder, if he doesn't run out of supplies, he can accomplish a great deal more during a normal workday. Don't underestimate the advantages to the professional of having a gofer on the premises. In case you aren't familiar with this term, it just means someone who goes for coffee, goes for nails, goes for a hammer. Granted, you won't find the job particularly creative, but the money savings will be yours.

Contractor: One step up the scale and you're out of the do-it-yourself realm. In the event you're genuinely edgy about taking on any of this work, this might be the most workable course for you. Scout about until you find a contractor with a good local reputation. That means he should have done work in the neighborhood that you can actually inspect. Talk to people for whom he worked. Find out if the job was satisfactory, if it was completed on time, if he stayed within price estimates.

In any event, don't necessarily go with the first contractor you see. Instead talk to several of them and get estimates from them. When you've narrowed your selection down to one or two candidates, ask them to submit written bids with cost estimates.

Seriously investigate the work these men have done in your neighborhood. Go over their bids very carefully. When you finally reach agreement, do so with a signed contract that details precisely the work that will be performed, lists the cost for this, and includes a date for completion.

Don't be carried away with the thought that you now have complete security. You don't really, because you can destroy it easily. All you have to do is make changes from the agreed bid and estimate. Just enlarge the terrace a bit, include a flat roof over one section, add some brick-edged flower-beds. Technically, any one of these changes can destroy the entire contractual agreement. In practical application, it would probably take a little more than this, but it is quite possible to toss the whole plan out the window.

The moral is simple: either stick rigidly to the agreed definition of the project or incorporate the changes in a new and separate agreement. In either event, you will be preserving the effectiveness of your original contract.

Architect: For a top-of-the-line professionally created and built project, this is most likely your best avenue. But you should understand that you pay for all the professional help that you get. However, if the design and planning of the deck, patio, or terrace is beyond you, and if you shudder at the thought of trying your hand at the actual construction, here's the solution: get an architect-designer, who will consider your desires, dreams, and fantasies, but only if practical; or get free plans from a local lumber yard; and remember resale of your house—don't go overboard on odd structure.

As with the contractor, ask around until you've located a professional architect who has a good reputation in the neighborhood. You want someone who has done work nearby, has completed the job successfully, and has stayed pretty close to the estimate in both time and money. When you have two or three candidates, talk to people for whom each has done work.

In addition to asking technical questions about the quality of the work performed, be sure to inquire if each was sensitive to the desires and lifestyle of the customers. Sad to say, a great many architects are seeking design triumphs instead of looking to satisfy customers. Their ideas may not be entirely bad, and you have probably seen the finished results in the pages of the many house-magazines. But, no matter how beautiful, if the finished project bears little relationship to the needs and desires of the people who commissioned it, the final effect is a sorry one.

Although this happens much more frequently with house-building, it applies to any type of home-construction project. The moral here is a simple one: know what you want,

Two decks: in the foreground, concrete steps bound with railroad ties leading past the elm from the living room to a deck that is bordered by benches. It connects by the strip-concrete walk with a dining deck in the rear, by the kitchen door.

Only a professional or a gifted amateur could design this so effectively, but any amateur carpenter could build it. It is always wise to have professional design ideas—the professionals will think of simple solutions for a complex of walls, heights, and trees.

An egg-crate shadow-casting roof extending from a stick fence (left, rear), with a stouter fence at the back. The distinctiveness comes from the Japanese-style pond under the cantilevered deck, with lots of planters of blooming chrysanthemum. Not an impossible achievement, even on so small and gravelly an area.

and speak up firmly. If the architect you are considering does not have a sensitivity to your needs, look elsewhere.

An architect's services can include several different aspects. Generally, it starts with design. After talking with you, after looking at your potential site, he will probably come up with some rough sketches. Then he will prepare a set of more complete working drawings. Once these are prepared, the architect can go to the next step. He will be responsible for locating reliable contractors and getting bids from them. He will go over their proposals with you and help you select the best candidate for the job. Then when the work is actually underway, he or someone from his office will actually be responsible for supervising the construction. In other words, if the contract says the footing should be 3 feet deep, you can rest assured someone acting in your interest will determine that this specification is actually met.

The big disadvantage of this package is cost. Although architects usually work on a percentage of the cost of the total project in determining their fees, this is not always feasible for a small-scale job. From the architects' standpoint, however, it is true that they frequently occupy a great deal of time without sufficient financial reward when calculated on a percentage basis. So don't be at all dismayed if the architect asks for a set fee or a combination of the fee plus percentage. He has to be compensated fairly for his work, so regard it as a fact of life.

Government Assistance

If weather, climate control, and the orientation of your new living space is the primary problem for you, the United States Government will give you a hand in solving this. For example, if you'd like to know the overall weather pattern in your specific area, there's some quite concise data available to you for very little money. To get this, send 15¢ to NOAA (that stands for the National Oceanic and Atmospheric Administration). The address is National Climate Center, Federal Building, Asheville, North Carolina 28801.

When you send in your money, ask for the current Local Climatological Data, annual issue. Be sure to specify the exact area where you live. The same office sells this information on a monthly basis. A year's subscription costs $2 and includes the annual.

Additional sources for precise weather data include: (1) U.S. Weather Bureau offices; (2) Federal Aviation Administration branches; (3) local airport operation offices; (4) National Park Service, U.S. Forest Service (check the state forestry district offices, too, as well as ranger stations); (5) U.S. Coast Guard stations and district offices; (6) public power and utility companies; (7) municipal water districts; (8) city, county, and state road and highway maintenance departments (because they battle weather conditions, they frequently maintain files of information on this topic); (9) meteorology departments of colleges and universities; (10) county farm bureaus and agricultural extension agents.

The best source for locating the above offices is your telephone book. Many of them will be listed under state or federal government. If you run into problems, try the public library. They can frequently tell you who locally has this type of information.

To recap quickly, the factors that require your consideration are: sun and its direction, prevailing winds, rain, snow, sounds, visual elements, existing structures, including roads and streets, and finally, most important, your own individual needs, requirements, and desires.

3
All Kinds of Decks

Just as a bold gate and towering shrubs signify an unapproachable estate, so does the imaginatively designed deck give the aura of warmth and welcome. In a locale that is lit by an oppressive sun, a small shaded deck with chairs or benches can be inviting. Where cold, bitter winds blow, a deck that is open to the sun but screened off from winds offers rest and warmth.

There are all kinds of decks, however, and if privacy and seclusion are your preference you can find a deck to suit you. Stone walls are not the only boundary lines that make good neighbors. Sometimes only a thorny hedge

Instead of a straight line of brick stairs, this house presents a warm invitation to enter, with a surprising double level of Japanese-style decking where the family can breakfast in the early morning.

Left: A small rear-deck, a reading nest and chair, to look out on the garden of this small contemporary house.

A transparent wall that takes advantage of the neighbor's handsome planting, which creates shadows from the other side. The simple stick fence fills irregular panels.

Solid and intricate, this Chinese-style patio hides the deck beyond.

will discourage small invaders; but you may have to baffle the wind or install a beautifying fence or safety barrier around a pool.

A tiny Japanese deck with the little walk, or engawa, where the hostess can come out to greet a guest and together they can rest a moment. Such a "porch" overlooks the Teton peaks in Wyoming, where deep snows could smother a larger deck in winter.

The combinations of screens, decks, pools, paths, and shrubs are limitless. It is interesting to note that some of our best ideas for outdoor living have come from Japan—a crowded nation of gracious and hospitable people. Not only have we adapted many of their concepts for construction of decks, but we are indebted to them for their invention of handsome screens, sliding doors, and architectural designs that concentrate on an enclosed bit of beauty.

Tanning and Sunbathing

Soaking up the sun is high on the list of advantages for most people when they start to think about a deck, patio, or terrace. A sheltered spot with evergreen plantings or louvered windbreaks that fend off cool breezes can afford a touch of luxury that borders on the exotic. For unwinding, it's hard to beat a session of slow baking under the warm sun.

To get the full advantage of this lazy activity, you'll have to plan your construction with the sun in mind. Since it's never been known to stand still, if you don't orient your patio, deck, or terrace to take full advantage of Old Sol, you can wind up in the unhappy position of catching only a short period of direct sunlight. Even worse, you may inadvertently find that you constantly have to shift mattress, book, and suntan lotion just to stay in the path of the sun—hardly a relaxing situation by anybody's standard.

At the same time, it might be necessary to have a deck or patio with both sun and shade. Your guests will probably differ in what they like. Some people can't take the sun at all, because of sensitive skin or eyes. Some are simply city people unused to all that exposure to brightness, and they will head straight for the chairs and table in a shaded corner.

Close to the Garden and Plants

If gardening is your particular delight, a patio, deck, or terrace can give you the opportunity to add an entirely new dimension to your green-thumb activities. Most gardens and planting areas are calculated for mass effect. The plants are banked in such a way that you don't really get that close to them. The colors are calculated to make a splash in large areas.

But if you've got a deck, you've got a grand new opportunity to create a close-up garden, where you will be right next to the plants. Quite likely they will be in tubs, raised pots, or planters; and, for this reason, anyone

Two rugged, rough fences in the West, where pretty fences would hardly blend in with lush vegetation and glaring sun.

*Contemporary deck, contemporary home, but with
traditional engawa (walkway) under a narrow roof.
Bright southern sun exposure for sunlovers, but with
overhangs that will completely shade the glass walk in
the height of summer, yet permit the slanting rays of
winter sun to penetrate the house. (The stout railing
with wire is obviously intended to keep the very
young from falling off.)*

*A shaded weekend house for owners who find the
bright sun hard on the eyes and skin. The wide railing
and seats are not difficult to build, and the old
Australian pine coming through the deck is the
greatest boon of all.*

*Cushions on a deck corner, for close-up view of bright-
leaved begonias that need no sun, with a strategically
placed potted bromeliad in bloom (upper left).*

*Dramatic night-lit garden with a small, simple
conversation-deck and tricky screen.*

who sees these shrubs or flowers will be aware of them as individual growing things. This can afford a fresh new approach, a tangent from any gardening you've done before. For the first time you have the opportunity to select a very few prime specimens, the most interesting ones, to feature in a setting that will enhance their beauty. For any home gardener this can be a delightful change of pace. However, in order to take full advantage of this new situation, the display areas, raised tubs, and sunken planters must all be planned for long before the first nail gets driven home.

Wooden Paths—Engawa

The deck path was originated by the Japanese many dynasties ago. Called an "engawa," it was usually constructed alongside a building to connect rooms under a roof. Today the term "engawa" is popular with architects to refer to a deck that is connected with the house or with another deck, or to refer to a series of narrow decks that lead off into a garden or toward the beach. A less pretentious term for this, used at beaches and resorts like Atlantic City or in the Old West, was "boardwalk."

To be precise, however, the term "engawa" applies only to the deck path alongside the house or in the garden.

The Outdoor Living Room

When you try to figure out the purpose you want your new outdoor living space to serve, consider it in terms of the rooms you now have inside your home. Are you looking for an extension of your indoor living room? If so, do try to figure out what you like about your current living room, as well as what you don't like. In planning your outdoor living room, you can accentuate the good things and possibly avoid blunders, such as lack of light or too close proximity to neighbors.

Privacy may seem a strange word to emphasize in the context of outdoor living, but it is a factor almost everyone needs. Try to decide what type of privacy is most important to you. Do you want to be shielded from the

A simple, rugged tree bench with roughly made legs.

The ancient shrine at Kyoto, Japan, with one of its engawa. Many consider this the most beautiful building in the world.

A deck and path with artful plantings, stones, and even young evergreens coming through the 2x2 lumber deck. This close to the ground, it would be wise to use the most effective preservative, though the material here is redwood.

Curved engawa (with staggered edges) leading to a circular sundeck in the garden.

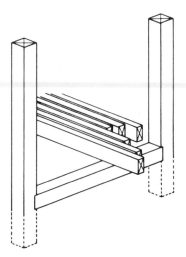

A contemporary, yet traditional engawa, leading from house to deck some distance away, past a garden of stones and a specimen evergreen.

Here the easy access to the living room, the wide, wide seats for crosslegged sitting, the series of steps down to the lawn level, and a large grill at the back wall could cook up a party for a junior-high-school class.

Interesting variation on the Japanese theme. The bridge on the far side is plain, without railing; the round stepping stones, traditional; and the near path and steps are unusual—made of vertical 2x6s fitted to the rocks.

This garden walk must be thoroughly coated with epoxy to keep the boards from buckling.

An intimate dining spot on a deck screened with decorative walls, and with corridor-like plantings appearing through the floor, creates the most secluded setting imaginable.

A tiny deck for two, just off the kitchen, could be turned into a banquet area for a wedding when the redwood top of the firepit in the foreground is uncovered and the family gathers round to cook for visitors.

scrutiny of passersby? Do you need complete privacy (such as for nude sunbathing)? Or will you be content with scattered foliage that acts as a partial barrier without totally blocking out all view?

Dining Out—at Home

The same applies to a dining room. For quite awhile, most families went along with the contemporary trend of having the dining room part of the living room. The reasoning was, "after all, we only use the space a few hours a day, and the rest of the time it's idle and wasted." All very well—but this reasonable attitude fails to take into account the desire most people have for order and privacy. Wasted space or not, a dining room is quite pleasant to have, if only because you can get up from the table and leave the dishes sitting until it's convenient to tidy up. In the living room you're either forced to sit with the clutter, which is not so pleasant, or be compelled to clear things away, which can be an intrusion on sociability.

So dining rooms are on the way back in. However, there might be a very workable intermediate solution. For example, a small terrace or deck right outside the kitchen door could have very pleasant dining prospects, depending on the climate of your locale. The cost would be only a fraction of that required to knock out walls, build full-scale foundations, and construct permanent roof, windows, and doors.

Planning is the most important ingredient of any new building project you tackle. So, before you head for the lumberyard, and even before you start drawing up plans, devote some time to quiet orderly thinking. There are several questions to be answered before kicking off any actual construction work.

Can the new space really serve as a dining area? The requirements for this are reasonable proximity to the kitchen, plus sufficient square footage in the proper configuration to accommodate a dining table, chairs, benches, and so forth. You will also need space for dishes and other accessories. Are you going to do any cooking there? If so, now is the time to think about making provision for barbecue grill, electric hotplate, warming trays, and perhaps water.

How much storage space will you require? Are you going to have cabinets to hold the outdoor dishes and silverware? Or will you store these in the kitchen? Are the table and the chairs going to be left there, or do you prefer furniture that folds away when not in use? If the latter is true, you'll need a place to stow all that stuff.

Entertaining a Lot of Guests

For some people, outdoor living-space is synonymous with partying and entertaining. It's hard to conceive of any area that is better suited to the purpose. You will probably furnish an outdoor space with an assortment of rugged furniture that is forgiving of spills, scuffs, soil, shoes or cigarette ashes—which means that your parties will be a lot more carefree for the host and hostess and that your guests will react well to the lack of tension. Generally, it will add up to a better, more enjoyable time for everyone.

If parties are your purpose, fine; but here again, don't neglect plenty of advance planning. For example, you might want a bar built into your new entertaining space, perhaps with storage space for glasses. Or you might have other possible needs for outdoor dining—i.e., tables and chairs, food storage space, serving facilities, or running water.

Beyond the big considerations, there are a whole host of smaller conveniences that can add greatly to the pleasure you'll get from your new space. However, these too require some advance planning.

For example if you are going to use the area for extensive dining, entertaining or large-scale gardening efforts, you may want to include a sink in the layout. If so, you'll definitely have to give thought to providing water and drainage lines. Obviously this feature is far simpler to obtain if there are already pipes in the house near the spot where you want the outdoor sink. Lighting and weatherproof outdoor outlets, as well as provisions

More than a little thought has gone into this deck. The bed-wide padded seats, the broad steps, and the wide passage off to the right to a lower area easily give elbow-room to lively teenagers who could party here without boredom. Hefty movable cushions hung from the wallboards can be slung down anywhere.

The deck of this country house extends far beyond the living quarters, wandering down to another level among the trees. A grill and setting for cocktails far from the house on deck and lawn will draw the guests away into conversational groups. If serving is done beside the house, guests will remain collected there.

A swimming pool, like thousands of others installed above ground level, is greatly enhanced by a wide lounging area and sauna-sized seat made of Douglas fir 2x4s easily cut to fit the gentle curve of the pool. Weathered planks are not slippery, don't retain heat, are glare-free, and drain and dry quickly. The uneven terrain of the ground beneath the deck was of no importance, as every deck can be leveled, and the required protecting wall does not have to be 10 feet high if the edge of the deck is 5 feet and more off the ground.

Better than the quiet pool, perhaps, is the garden fountain (recirculating, no doubt). But the circular motif here astonishes with pleasure—the round dish basin, one round deck overpassing another round deck of equal size, and the low round marbletopped table in the center. Difficult to build for a first-timer, but even more demanding in design, yet no architect is found on the credits. The gardener is a person of experience.

A lakehouse without a deck is an anachronism. Ask any suburban or country lumberyard manager why he is selling so much lumber in a time of self-restricted building, and he will tell you that it is going for deck building, whether on dry land, around a pool, or on a lake. The extra bedrooms are postponed, because they raise taxes. The new deck doesn't. Keeping up with the aquatic Joneses next door means that your neighbor will say, "I don't know why I didn't build a deck as big as yours while I was at it."

for a hi-fi system, should not be tacked on at the last minute. Instead, figure out where you will want built-in light- or convenience-outlets so you can incorporate them in the construction.

A sunshade, an awning, or a roll-up roof can add extra utility to the area and extend the pleasure you'll get from it. These too should not be afterthoughts. Make them a part of the overall design so that structurally, as well as aesthetically, you will wind up with a workable and a beautiful adjunct to your home. (By the way, they are essential if you are planning outdoor sleeping.)

Water Living

For some, a view of water is a necessity of life. Every gardener dreams of a pool, and most will do anything to get one. A lucky few may have a pond or a reasonable facsimile of one. For Los Angelinos, it is obvious that nothing less than a swimming pool will do. From the air, flying over the 500-square-miles of Los Angeles suburbs, one is struck not so much by oil wells or throughways as by the thousands of pools of every conceivable size and shape. Yet on the ground most of them are hidden by fencing.

A craze for beaches threatens the politics of every urban administration in America, and hardly a community fails to support at least one public pool. No private golf club would dare to be without its own pool. And, where lakes are not natural—either as big as the Great Lakes or as small as Lake Tahoe—rivers are dammed and lakes are made. And every river has its community pressure group to keep it as clean as possible, from the Hudson to the Savannah, to the riverbeds of California and sparkling waters of the Northwest. Every dock is a deck for the young and foolhardy. And where there is no deck, one is now being built or dreamed of.

Up in the Sky and Treetops

High decks are a concept calculated to bring migraines to home-handymen. Once you get up above an easy distance from the

Beauty on the lake. Wide 2x8 planks laid down with 2x6s in checkerboard design leading under this lovely semitropical tree, across the bridge that also provides a dinghy harbor, to the slant-backed benches that make the deck seem lighter. For gazing, for eating, for fishing, sunning, and swimming, and for a group of friends to come together at night and drift apart.

At the shore, there is nothing to make you feel more at home than a boardwalk. But it need not be a string of boards. Here is a checkerboard design of 2x6 planks and box seats keeping back the sand, with double 2x12s leading from a wide deck and wandering into a narrowing irregular walk down to a retaining wall well above high tide. Designed by an architect.

Beside a pond of water lilies and water hyacinths, a handsome deck covered with a gently-curving, smooth plastic roof that runs under and over the rafters. The reed fencing gives complete privacy. There is an accent of reeds growing in the pond and from the rocks below, a climbing plant, the purple heart (Setcreasea purpurea), a close cousin of the wandering Jew.

You don't expect the reed fence to last more than a few seasons; it can change to something else equally inexpensive and soft-textured.

Not a usual swimming pool: the deck made of 4x4s, above pebbled concrete, a weeping cedar in a formal bed of river stones. The garden, with a greenhouse in the rear, makes the pool a less dominant feature.

ground, the construction problems multiply. Foundations to support the rig become heavier, larger, and more involved. Even the otherwise relatively simple job of getting to the work involves scaffolding. By any handyman's standards, it's time-consuming and expensive. But once up, admittedly there are pleasures: one can look not down on the trees and not up at them, but through their branches. If the slope of ground drops off steeply from your terrace or deck foundations, you have it easy. Your deck foundation posts can be only 4 to 6 feet high, yet a few feet away from your deck rail you see migrating birds that perch 30-feet-up in your trees.

A Deck Guest Room?

Are you really thinking of an extension to your bedroom? Many people have found that a deck situated adjacent to the bedroom completely shifts the use pattern. Instead of the room being utilized for sleeping only, it becomes a private sitting room as well. And private is a good word. With the only entrance to the area through the bedroom, it doesn't function as a general lounging section for the rest of the family or for guests.

Also, with sufficient planning for privacy and storage, you can get away without tacking on that additional guest room that has always seemed so essential. Depending upon climate and the attitudes of your houseguests (if they are younger or if they are outdoor types) a sort of sunporch deck (or patio or terrace) might answer that need a good portion of the time.

In many parts of the country, with the lifestyle that quite a few people prefer nowadays, a deck can frequently serve double-duty as a guest bedroom.

Okay, so it may not have complete privacy (depending on the plans) and its use may be restricted by the climate and the weather. Just the same, when your kids bring home a pack of friends on the spur-of-the-moment and ask if they can sleep over, it can be a godsend to be able to stash them in some place other than the living room—which may

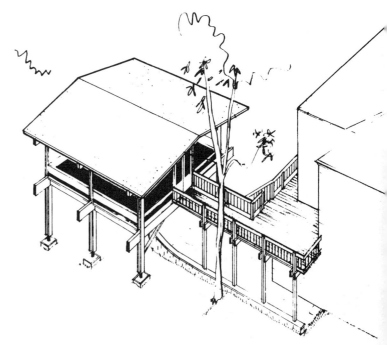

A delightful second-story screenhouse connected to the house by two engawa or deckpaths. The owners did not wish to build onto the house and darken windows, but also did not want to descend a flight to an outside living room/dining room/bedroom. Three children aided the architect, and with a central cooking and storage area (including running water), the handsome roofed, screened house has everything that a large screened porch rarely provides— including drama.

The architect's sketch shows its relationship to the house.

An open redwood deck, providing strolling and sitting area off two bedrooms, both with roll-down nighttime stargazing, and outdoor sleeping, in a mild climate that is generally dry.

have *no* privacy. Keep a stock of sleeping bags on hand (though they usually bring their own), murmur a soft prayer for good weather, and you'll be in fine shape to cope with this influx. If it rains, a roll-down canvas awning will add to the joy of sleep.

As for guests in an age-bracket beyond the younger set, the whole situation may become a little "iffy." Some people will be perfectly charmed with the idea of bedding down in the outdoors. For others, the situation can loom as a profound breach of hospitality. If your houseguests are the kind of people who might find this idea attractive, fold-up bed facilities in weatherproof storage cabinets built into the deck could easily save the cost of adding on an extra bedroom. And a patio canvas roof will keep them dry.

A bird's-eye-view of a completely private bedroom deck. Screened by a vine trellis immediately below and at the opposite end, bordered by a broad planting box along the outer edge, the suburban hostess leads guests through her bedroom for talk outside. Loving the fresh cool air, she and her husband often sleep there. The deck includes a telephone extension.

A second-story deck often adds dignity to the architecture of the house and provides here a large area off two bedrooms, both with roll-down shades. This one is made of redwood. Along the railing are planters with large plants providing privacy. A large family of relatives or a college crowd can be provided for.

This is a perfect lounging place night and day. Perhaps this would bring relief to the insomniac.

4
The Materials for the Job

From many viewpoints and certainly from a practical standard, it's virtually impossible to beat the economy and ease of construction you get with that standby, wood. It will support more weight in proportion to its own weight than most other materials. It can be cut, shaped, glued, fastened together, and fabricated into virtually any configuration you want. Just by heading for the lumberyard and by picking from the vast assortment available there, you can have an incredible variety of options in terms of shapes, patterns, and so forth. Get a brush and a can of paint, stain, oil, or bleach, and you've escalated the possibilities another notch.

Different Woods

The type of lumber you buy depends to a large extent on the section of the country where you live. For example, on the west coast, redwood is generally available and relatively inexpensive. The same wood in the east may cost more, and you may have to find a bargain by contacting several lumberyards. In the south, cypress is not too prohibitive in cost. In the north and the east, the most generally available hardwood is fir. All these are relatively suitable for construction of decks, raised patios, and such. Hemlock, spruce, white pine, lodgepole pine, sugar pine, ponderosa pine, western larch, and cedar are also available for a variety of wood-building projects.

Wood Dimensions: You will probably do most of the basic framing for your deck, patio, or terrace with what's called dimensional lumber. That simply means it comes in set sizes. The most common is 2x4 lumber. Similar pieces of wood are available in sizes such as 2x2, 2x3, 2x6, 2x8, 2x10, and 2x12. Moving up the line, heavier timbers come 4x4, 4x6, 4x8, and so forth. Even larger are 6x6s and 8x8s. The larger sizes are not always readily available, however. No need to fret though. It is possible to construct a heavy timber by nailing or bolting together two smaller timbers of equal size. These can be used as beams under a deck where, unseen, you want strength, not perfection. For example, a couple of 2x10s make a 4x10. Or a pair of 2x4s become a 4x4 timber.

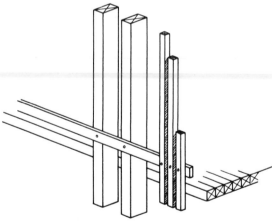

Twin laminated 2x3s were used here. The uprights are wood fiberboard ¼ inch thick. Low-grade lumber (utility or #3 light framing) was used for the horizontal 2x4 supports, with the best edge for the top of the railing. For decking, 2x3s on edge were used. (For plans, see Sources of Supplies.)

Some lumberyards and building-supply companies carry natural poles. These range all the way from small sticks to good-size logs. For the most part they're available either with the bark in place or peeled for the rustic look.

In the jargon of the lumber trade, lengths of wood that are both wider and thicker than 5 inches and have the surfaces planed or "dressed" are called timbers. When you get up into the heavier varieties, the cost rises proportionately. Also the jumbo timbers, along with the large diameter poles, are brutally heavy. Just hefting them into position requires a platoon of your friends.

Grades of Lumber—and Some Warnings: It's probably good to learn a bit of the jargon before you head for the lumberyard, so that you'll be able to converse meaningfully with the guy behind the counter. However, do be prepared for the fact that you may not be able to get precisely what you want. Availability of specific lumber grades and types varies considerably according to the economic tenor of the times plus the area of the country where you live. So some of the finer considerations may turn out to be largely academic. But don't let this throw you. If you deal with a local supplier whose livelihood depends upon treating you well enough so that you will walk in that front door time and time again, you will probably wind up with perfectly acceptable substitutes.

One other point: sometimes, although you can get precisely what you want, the cost can shake the morale of a potentate. Carefully explain to the people at the supply company what you're going to use the various materials for. They will probably be in a position to guide you and, in the process, perhaps save some money for you.

Generally, use the kind of wood that's most available in your section of the country. Earlier, it was mentioned that redwood, for example, is easily obtained in the western part of the United States. If you want to buy this wood in the east, it's available, but at a higher cost. In the east you'll be far better off sticking to fir, which is plentiful and relatively inexpensive. This is a subject where your local lumberyard can be very helpful in guiding you.

Don't buy a fancier or higher grade of lumber than you really need for a particular part of the job. Sure a terrace would be beautiful constructed of clear, #1-grade lumber, but the cost could have you filing for bankruptcy. Quite likely most of your work will be done with construction-grade lumber or an even lower category known as standard. This means the wood will have knots and defects, so that it won't be overly pretty, and should be strong enough for the supports and joists out of sight. But the deck surface has to be smooth. Don't buy low-grade lumber for deck surfacing in 2x4s or 2x6s.

Meaning of Sizes: The sizing of wood can be confusing until you get the hang of it and understand the system used. For example, a 2x4 does not measure 2 inches by 4 inches. At one point in the process from tree to timber, it did. That is, when the piece of wood was rough-sawn from the log, the result of that first cutting was 2 inches by 4 inches. After that the wood was dried; and, in the process, it shrank, and then it was surfaced or milled smooth on the sides. As a result of all this treatment the 2x4s you buy in the lumberyard actually measure 1½ inches by 3½ inches. This same routine applies for other sizes of lumber: 2x6s, 2x8s, 4x4s, and so forth.

Surfacing is another variation. If all four sides of the board are planed smooth, it's known as S4S. Theoretically it's possible to buy lumber that's planed on only one side S1S, or two sides S2S. But don't count on this. In these days of spiralling prices, you may have to take what's available in your price category. However, if you can get by with lumber that is smooth on 1 side only, the cost will be slightly less.

Stick with stock sizes when you buy lumber. If you want an oddball dimension that is not in the regular catalog, many lumberyards will cut it to order for you. However, you remember, you pay for the wood according to the original size plus an additional charge for cutting.

This same holds true for lumber in nonstandard lengths. According to the book, you should be able to buy lumber in lengths from 8 to 20 feet in 1-foot increments. However, most lumberyards carry few stock sizes,

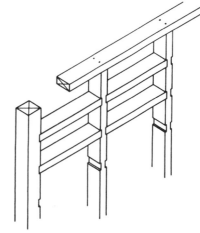

The 4x4 posts of this contemporary fence are red cedar heartwood, free of heart-center and sapwood. Without treatment, it resists decay when embedded in concrete or earth. Almost all other woods require preservative. (For plans see Sources of Supplies.)

Old weathered railroad ties make perfect step and terraced slopes. Not all are tarred and blackened, and even these can be cleaned up. Lumberyards are selling well-surfaced ties that can be stained to give the effect of great beams no one would suspect of coming from the old railroad.

and they're limited to the lumber they can sell easily. This means that you can buy 2x4s in 8-, 12-, and sometimes 16-foot lengths, but you may have to do some searching if you want longer sizes or if you want lengths in between these dimensions. As a matter of fact, the quickest way to get drummed out of the store is to ask for something like a 13-foot length of lumber. If your request is honored, the wood, in most cases, will be cut from the next larger available size (for which you will be charged).

Character of Wood: Another pair of lumber terms are "heartwood" and "sapwood." These names refer to the part of the tree from which the wood was cut. Heartwood comes from the center portion of the tree, sapwood from the area near the bark. Generally heartwood is more resistant to decay, while sapwood will soak up preservatives, stain, and such, in a more satisfactory manner. Once again don't depend on merely stating your request to get either heartwood or sapwood. For the most part, lumberyards don't differentiate. If there's a special reason for your needing one particular variety, and if you're a good customer, they may scurry around a bit to accommodate your request. However,

these days such actions come under the category of a favor.

Discount and Shopping Around: If you're tackling a particularly large job and will be using a considerable amount of lumber, there is a ploy you might try. When you first visit the lumberyard, show them the plans and the lumber list. Explain that you are doing the job yourself and ask if they will extend to you a contractor's discount. It all depends on how hungry they are for new business or how eager they are to accommodate you. In some cases you may be accorded a discount of 5 or 10 percent, or perhaps even more. In any event, there's no harm in asking.

One other source of saving is to consolidate all of your purchases. Place the order all at one time and, if possible, have it delivered all at one time. When you do so, explain that this is your purpose. If the lumberyard knows that they won't have to service your materials list on a stick-by-stick basis, or have to send a truck out to deliver a few boards every other day, they may be more inclined to extend price courtesy to you. At the same time you buy lumber, check to see if the yard can extend satisfactory prices to you on such other materials as nails, hardware, paint, and

Table 1. Minimum Post Sizes (Wood Beam Supports)[1]

Species group[2]	Post size (in.)	Load area[3] beam spacing x post spacing (sq. ft.)									
		36	48	60	72	84	96	108	120	132	144
1	4x4	Up to 12-ft. heights →				Up to 10-ft. heights →			Up to 8-ft. heights →		
	4x6					Up to 12-ft. heights →				Up to 10-ft. →	
	6x6									Up to 12-ft. →	
2	4x4	Up to 12-ft. →		Up to 10-ft. hts. →			Up to 8-ft. heights →				
	4x6			Up to 12-ft. hts. →			Up to 10-ft. heights →				
	6x6						Up to 12-ft. heights →				
3	4x4	Up to 12′	Up to 10′ →		Up to 8-ft. hts. →			Up to 6-ft. heights →			
	4x6		Up to 12′ →		Up to 10-ft. hts. →			Up to 8-ft. heights →			
	6x6			Up to 12-ft. heights →							

[1] Based on 40 p.s.f. deck live load plus 10 p.s.f. dead load. Grade is Standard and Better for 4x4-inch posts and No. 1 and Better for larger sizes.

[2] Group 1—Douglas fir, larch and southern pine; Group 2—Hem fir, and Douglas fir south; Group 3—Western pine and cedar, redwood, and spruce.

[3] Example: If the beam supports are spaced 8 feet, 6 inches, on center and the posts are 11 feet, 6 inches, on center, then the load area is 98. Use next larger area 108.

so forth. If you're visiting a large building-supply company, you may even want to pick up your tools at the same place. Again the idea is to bulk your purchases so that you will be in a position to give a fairly large order to one company. This gives you a little leverage in requesting a discount.

Don't neglect scrounging as a source of materials. The list of possibilities includes lumber reclaimed from old buildings, as well as materials purchased from construction projects. This last can be a veritable goldmine: when large-scale construction projects are finished, there is frequently a vast amount of surplus materials, including wood, planks, timbers, and even some steel girders.

Unless the contractor is ready to start another job immediately, it's frequently a nuisance for him to take these materials back to a warehouse and store them until they're needed again. This means that you can pick them up for very little money. Of course they will be damaged, dirty, or otherwise less than totally desirable; but, if you're willing to spend a little extra work cleaning up the surfaces, you can certainly trim your construction budget considerably.

Types of Lumber

Here is a not-so-complicated chart put out by the United States Forest Service (Handbook No. 432, "Construction Guides for Exposed Wooden Decks"). It takes into account the bearing strength of all the common types of lumber, and shows what measurement of span is safe for each type and use. It is worthwhile studying the figures for the type of lumber available at lowest cost in your part of the country with their grades. Once you learn what is available to you, check that type of lumber to learn what size is suitable for posts, beams, joists, and deck.

Preservatives

For rot-resistance, various woods can be treated with any one of several available preservatives. Copper naphthenate is a popular one, and it's available under several different brand names. However, it is deep green in color and stains the wood this shade. This is fine if the timber is going to be below ground or concealed—or if you happen to want a green patio. Otherwise the color can be an intrusion.

Zinc naphthenate, a similar chemical, can

afford the same rot-resistant properties, but it has the advantage of being transparent. It is, however, more expensive than copper naphthenate.

Although you will get some effectiveness by brushing on a coat of either preservative, the most effective treatment is to soak the wood for several days or perhaps a week in a solution of preservative. To accomplish this, most home carpenters construct a crude box large enough to contain the lengths of wood, line it with polyethylene film, and fill it with preservative. The timbers are merely soaked in this until they absorb enough of the solution to take on some rot-resistant properties.

However, unless you're building for the ages or have some special moisture conditions present, there's generally no need to go to such lengths. Woods such as redwood, cypress, and fir have certain rot-resistant properties built right into them, courtesy of nature. As long as you utilize an open type of construction, in which any water can run down and out, you're relatively safe proceeding with construction without bothering to rot-proof all the individual pieces of wood in the job.

Table 2. Minimum Beam Sizes and Spans[1]

Species group[2]	Beam size (in.)	\[Spacing between beams[3] (ft.)\] 4	5	6	7	8	9	10	11	12
1	4x6	Up to 6-ft. spans →								
	3x8	Up to 8-ft. →		Up to 7' →	Up to 6-ft. spans →					
	4x8	Up to 10'	Up to 9' →	Up to 8' →	Up to 7-ft. →	Up to 6-ft. spans →				
	3x10	Up to 11'	Up to 10' →	Up to 9' →	Up to 8-ft. →		Up to 7-ft. →		Up to 6-ft. →	
	4x10	Up to 12'	Up to 11' →	Up to 10' →	Up to 9-ft. →		Up to 8-ft. →		Up to 7-ft. →	
	3x12		Up to 12' →	Up to 11' →	Up to 10' →	Up to 9-ft. →		Up to 8-ft spans →		
	4x12			Up to 12-ft. →		Up to 11' →	Up to 10-ft. →		Up to 9-ft. →	
	6x10				Up to 12' →		Up to 11' →	Up to 10-ft. spans →		
	6x12						Up to 12-ft. spans →			
2	4x6	Up to 6-ft. →								
	3x8	Up to 7-ft. →		Up to 6-ft. →						
	4x8	Up to 9'	Up to 8' →	Up to 7-ft. →		Up to 6-ft. →				
	3x10	Up to 10'	Up to 9' →	Up to 8' →	Up to 7-ft. →		Up to 6-ft. spans →			
	4x10	Up to 11'	Up to 10' →	Up to 9' →	Up to 8-ft. →		Up to 7-ft. spans →		Up to 6' →	
	3x12	Up to 12'	Up to 11' →	Up to 10' →	Up to 9' →	Up to 8-ft. →		Up to 7-ft. spans →		
	4x12		Up to 12' →	Up to 11' →	Up to 10-ft. →		Up to 9-ft. →		Up to 8-ft. →	
	6x10			Up to 12' →	Up to 11' →	Up to 10-ft. →		Up to 9-ft. spans →		
	6x12				Up to 12-ft. spans →			Up to 11-ft. →	Up to 10'	
3	4x6	Up to 6'								
	3x8	Up to 7'	Up to 6' →							
	4x8	Up to 8'	Up to 7' →	Up to 6-ft. →						
	3x10	Up to 9'	Up to 8' →	Up to 7' →	Up to 6-ft. spans →					
	4x10	Up to 10'	Up to 9' →	Up to 8-ft. →		Up to 7-ft. →	Up to 6-ft. spans →			
	3x12	Up to 11'	Up to 10' →	Up to 9' →	Up to 8' →	Up to 7-ft. spans →			Up to 6-ft. →	
	4x12	Up to 12'	Up to 11' →	Up to 10' →	Up to 9-ft. →		Up to 8-ft. →		Up to 7-ft. →	
	6x10		Up to 12' →	Up to 11' →	Up to 10' →	Up to 9-ft. →		Up to 8-ft spans →		
	6x12			Up to 12-ft. →		Up to 11-ft. →	Up to 10-ft. →		Up to 8' →	

[1] Beams are on edge. Spans are center to center distances between posts or supports. (Based on 40 p.s.f. deck live load plus 10 p.s.f. dead load. Grade is No. 2 or Better; No. 2 medium grain southern pine.)
[2] Group 1—Douglas fir, larch and southern pine; Group 2—Hem fir and Douglas fir south; Group 3—Western pine and cedar, redwood, and spruce.
[3] Example: If the beams are 9 feet, 8 inches, apart and the species is Group 2, use the 10-ft. column; 3x10 up to 6-ft. spans, 4x10 or 3x12 up to 7-ft. spans, 4x12 or 6x10 up to 9-ft. spans, 6x12 up to 11-ft. spans.

Footings, Climate, and Foundation Heave

Cold weather can be much more of a hazard on the deck or terrace than on your guests.

If the ground on which you want to build is rocky and uneven, a deck is the simplest "level ground" you can create. But if the foundation earth is marshy or unstable, give serious thought to shifting to a better locale. Some types of soil simply will not support the foundation needed for columns or posts without a great deal of preparatory work. Beside a stream or lake or on marshy land, where there are heavy freezes, you have to have foundation posts below the freezing level or your new deck or patio will heave up 5 or 6 inches in freezing temperatures. In such cases you may have to dig down and go below the freezing level, normally 3 feet deep in northern states. In other unhappy circumstances, you may have to rent the services of a pile driver (let's hope not!) if you hope to end up with a sufficiently rugged foundation for your new construction. While none of this is impossible, it does constitute an additional drain on time and money.

If a change of site will eliminate this hassle, try to stay flexible enough to accept the shift. The other side of the house or garden may be free of problems.

Concrete Foundation Posts: Concrete is becoming a popular material for the support, or "footings," of deckposts. (See drawing, page 42.) Surprisingly enough, it's a do-it-yourself situation. At most large lumberyards and building-supply companies, you can also buy fiber tube forms that are designed for pouring the concrete. (See drawing, page 51.) You set them in position in the ground and fill them with concrete, which you can buy ready-to-mix. It already has the proper proportion of sand, cement, gravel, lime, and so forth, in it. Just add the proper amount of water and mix the stuff together in a large bucket or rough cement "boat," nailed together from odds and ends of scrap lumber. After the mixture sets, you wind up with a post or column that won't burn, decay, or succumb to the ravages of termites.

Table 3. Maximum Allowable Spans for Deck Joists[1]

Species group[2]	Joist size (inches)	Joist spacing (inches)		
		16	24	32
1	2x6	9'-9"	7'-11"	6'-2"
	2x8	12'-10"	10'-6"	8'-1"
	2x10	16'-5"	13'-4"	10'-4"
2	2x6	8'-7"	7'-0"	5'-8"
	2x8	11'-4"	9'-3"	7'-6"
	2x10	14'-6"	11'-10"	9'-6"
3	2x6	7'-9"	6'-2"	5'-0"
	2x8	10'-2"	8'-1"	6'-8"
	2x10	13'-0"	10'-4"	8'-6"

[1] Joists are on edge. Spans are center to center distances between beams or supports. Based on 40 p.s.f. deck live load plus 10 p.s.f. dead load. Grade is No. 2 or Better; No. 2 medium grain southern pine.

[2] Group 1—Douglas fir, larch and southern pine; Group 2—Hem fir and Douglas fir south; Group 3—Western pine and cedar, redwood, and spruce.

Table 4. Maximum Allowable Spans for Spaced Deck Boards[1]

Species group[2]	Maximum allowable span (inches)[3]					
	Laid flat				Laid on edge	
	1x4	2x2	2x3	2x4	2x3	2x4
1	16	60	60	60	90	144
2	14	48	48	48	78	120
3	12	42	42	42	66	108

[1] These spans are based on the assumption that more than one floor board carries normal loads. If concentrated loads are a rule, spans should be reduced accordingly.

[2] Group 1—Douglas fir, larch and southern pine; Group 2—Hem fir and Douglas fir south; Group 3—Western pine and cedar, redwood, and spruce.

[3] Based on Construction grade or Better (Select Structural, Appearance, No. 1 or No. 2).

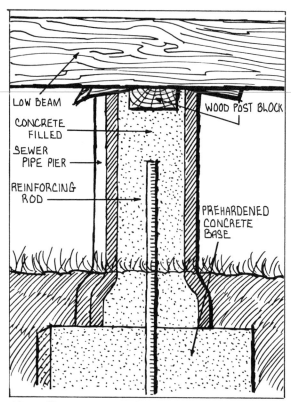

LOW BEAM

CONCRETE FILLED

SEWER PIPE PIER

REINFORCING ROD

WOOD POST BLOCK

PREHARDENED CONCRETE BASE

Above: Beam on sewer pipe concrete pier.

Below: Prefab concrete footing.

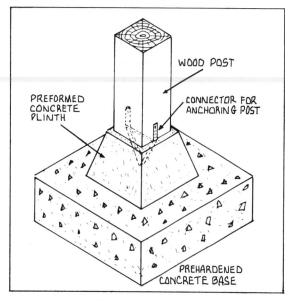

PREFORMED CONCRETE PLINTH

WOOD POST

CONNECTOR FOR ANCHORING POST

PREHARDENED CONCRETE BASE

Fiber tube forms are also available in various sizes ranging in diameter from 6 to 24 inches. Cost is figured by the foot of length. The fiber tube forms aren't intended to be permanent. Once you've filled them with concrete and the mixture has completely set, you peel away the form and discard it.

If the fiber tubes are not available locally, you can also use clay sewer pipe for this purpose. This comes in various diameters, generally ranging from 4 to 8 inches, and in several lengths, up to 5 feet. Use these in the same way you would use the fiber tubes, but you do not need to peel away the form once the concrete is set.

The main disadvantage of concrete is that the work of mixing and handling it is brutally hard. Added to this is the fact that the stuff is heavy, so that, if you fill a form in one place, it can take a mule team to lug it over to another site.

Engineers suggest that you restrict any type of poured concrete construction to a height of 3 feet or less.

Concrete Blocks: Reasonably lightweight, quite sturdy, and readily available, this material has proven to be the answer to a lot of foundation problems for homeowners all over the country. When the blocks are stacked one on top of the other and the core holes filled with concrete and reinforcing rods, the result is a rugged pier suitable for many foundation tasks. You can buy concrete blocks at most building-supply companies and lumberyards. Do make sure you buy a block known as "standard aggregate." A similar material is available in the form of cinderblocks, but these do not have the same strength.

Iron Pipe: Another possibility is iron-pipe posts. This stuff is much more expensive than wood or concrete and quite a bit harder to work with. However, it is rugged, and it does go up fast. If you need only a small amount of support for your deck, and if you have a building-supply company nearby that will cut the pipe to specification, it might be advisable to use this particular material. As for iron railings, you can come up with an interesting design to keep it from looking like a railroad station. However, the plumbing techniques required for using "elbows," male and female fittings (as the trade calls them), and for using the tool with which you thread every joint, are generally beyond the patience and possibly the strength of an amateur. Have a carpenter-plumber put up your iron-pipe railing and have it designed by an architect.

Iron railings are available everywhere

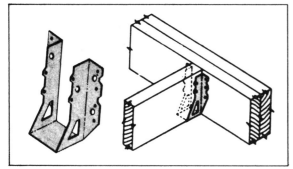

Hanger connecting joist and ledger board.

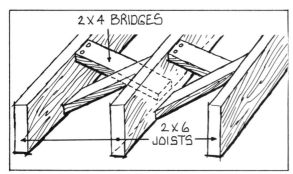

Joist bridging with wood.

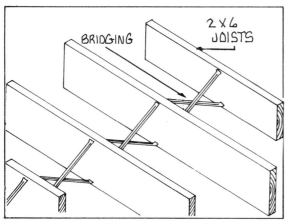

Metal joist bridging.

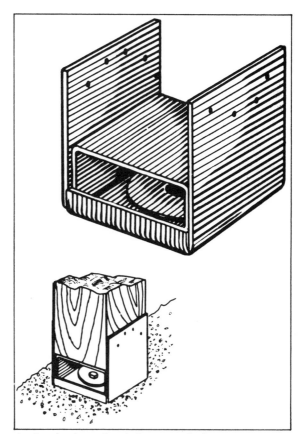

Anchor for fastening 4x4 posts to deck.

ready-made, or custom-made at your local ironworks. They are far more attractive than iron pipe.

Metal Framing Anchors: Without a doubt the greatest thing to come down the pike in recent years is the development of preformed metal anchor plates and clips. For the homeowner who just wants to get through some difficult construction job in the easiest way that will provide the strength and rigidity he needs, these little gadgets can be an absolute blessing. They are as simple as they are ingenious. The clips and plates are an odd assortment of bent and punched pieces of sheet metal. However, an enormous amount of design and engineering work has gone into the development of them. As a result they can speed the job without sacrificing any structural standards.

Several companies manufacture the metal connectors that hold wooden posts to con-

The narrow city backyard with high roughhewn fences can be decked perfectly. The boards used here were 4x4s. The short railings were designed to match the second-story ones of these row houses. The flagstone in the foreground sets off the border of flowers and bushes and leads to the second heavily built deck.

The opposite end of the same garden; the second deck is octagonal. Wooden steps lead to a higher garden area, and a unique iron gazebo. At night, the downward-lighted garden is subdued and quieting.

crete foundation footings, such as the prefab concrete "plinths." There are also "hangers" to join floor joists to the ledger boards of the house or to beams (either by joining joists to beam horizontally or holding the joist down to a beam below), as well as joining beams to each other. It is well to browse the catalogs of your favorite lumberyard dealer for these metal connectors. They require only nails, are little trouble, and are far easier to use than simply nailing one wood member to another (known as "toe-nailing").

You can construct your entire deck safely with these ingenious devices, if you can find the right one for a particular joining.

With metal connectors, you will be able to do a great deal of the work single-handedly. For example, the joist hangers can be partially nailed in position on the beams at either end of the flooring, and then the joists themselves can be lifted into the U-shaped clips, one end at a time. This is not the greatest system in the world, but it is certainly workable.

Other types of clips and metal hardware perform even more intricate tasks. For example, one variety combines a heavy-duty pipe-support with a U-shaped clip at the top. The supports are designed to be mounted within the concrete foundation, while the clips at the top hold the main wood supports for a deck. Other types of hardware are made specially to support a railing with safety and rigidity.

And if you'd like a quick and easy way to build some outdoor furniture, preformed metal sections are once again the answer. With them you can quickly construct benches, seats, tables, and other nifties. All it takes is the proper type of metal fitting plus dimensional lumber. The how-to of it all is detailed on pages 75–81.

Other Deck-Building Aids

Briefly, here's a quick run-down on the available items and what they can do.

For foundations, there's a V-shaped gizmo, used to attach wood beams or sills to a concrete-block pier or foundation.

A U-shaped joist-hanger does just what the name indicates. It will hold and support various-sized joists ranging from 2x4 to a pair of laminated 2x14s. As you know, the usual method involves a supporting metal bracket screwed to the wood members to be joined. The joist hanger in a number of forms is a vastly simpler solution.

Framing anchors are perfect for various types of studding applications. Once again there is no need to toe-nail because the preformed metal pieces are designed to hook in place with straight surface nailing. The same clip is usable where the stud meets the plate at the top as well as where it joins up with the sill at the bottom.

If you would prefer to have one piece of shaped metal that can tackle several different applications, there's one called an all-purpose framing anchor. You merely bend up certain sections of it to adapt it for various applications.

Other framing clips are used to hold up deck-rafters. Actually several different types of hardware will accomplish this task. Or you can adapt the all-purpose framing anchor.

For post-and-beam construction, another set of hardware pieces are specifically designed to speed the work. There is, for example, a preformed metal section designed to connect an upright post to a horizontal beam. A similar preformed plate does the same job but is designed to be fastened on one side of the assembly only.

At the bottom end of the post, a different metal gadget vastly simplifies the job of securing the upright posts to the base or foundation. What's more they hold the wood slightly raised above the surface as additional protection against moisture.

One fact should be emphasized with all of these metal connectors. They eliminate the need for toe-nailing various sections of wood timbers together. In the eyes of many traditional carpenters this may be heresy indeed, because toe-nailing has long been regarded as the standard method for securing many joints in house construction. However, it is not by any means the strongest method. More important, it's rather time-consuming.

Because these metal plates and connectors all fasten in position with surface nailing only, the application takes a fraction of the time required for toe-nailing. In addition, some of the metal gadgets (the joist hangers,

for example) result in greater strength and a far neater job.

The next chapter spells out how these materials are used on the actual site. The appendix details the tools that are used for wood deck-building, both hand tools and a few hand power-tools.

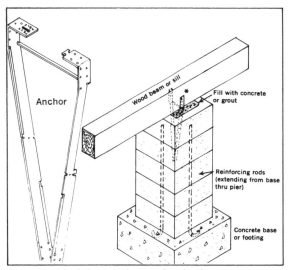

Concrete-block foundation anchor for beams.

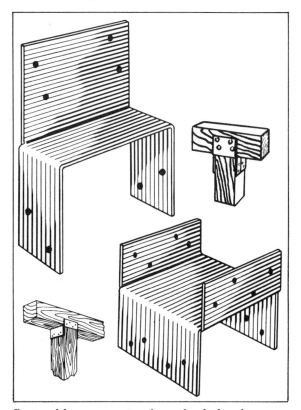

Post-and-beam connectors for under deck or for deck arbor.

5
Decks–How They Go Up

A terrace can give you a feeling of being at one with the earth, right there with nature. The overall impression afforded by a deck is slightly different. You get the same outdoor feeling but the height contributes an impression of open spaciousness. You are looking down or over, not just across.

These are vague, abstract concepts, to be sure. The first time you settle down on your deck with a book and a cold drink, you will immediately understand the appeal, however. Although decks are more difficult to build than terraces, they can overcome some serious problems of construction. For example, if your lot includes a bunch of huge boulders, if it slopes at a steep angle, if it is cut by a small stream, or if it is composed of loose or soggy earth that just won't support a terrace, a deck may be the only solution for you. Then, of course, there is the aesthetic factor: a raised deck can lift you up that slight extra amount so you can take advantage of a view.

The Parts

Like an old-time erector set, a deck goes together in segments or pieces. Briefly, here are the parts.

Ledger: The height of your deck is determined by the line along your house where the edge of your deck will be: 2 to 6 feet up, just under a door, or 10 feet up just under a second-story door or sliding glass panel. Along this line, you will nail to the wood or bolt to the masonry of your house a 2x6 or a 2x8 board the full length of the future deck. This board is known as the *facer* or *ledger*, and it can be made level by a carpenter's level.

Footing: This is the surface in contact with the ground. It is designed to support the foundation pier that fits on top of it. In all climates, the footings extend down to a solid surface, either rock or hard soil. In cold climates, where there's a problem with the temperature, footings should go all the way down below the frost line. The exact depth varies according to geographical location—usually 3 feet in deep-frost areas. The purpose is to start the primary supports of the deck at a point where they will not heave upward because of frost lifting the footings. Piers are generally pre-fab concrete, concrete block, or similar material. They fit on top of the footings and extend up to a point slightly above ground level.

Posts: These are generally made of wood or metal. They're positioned on top of the piers and are the main extension for the height of the deck, lifting it up to the desired position. (Posts are also the uprights above the deck, if any.)

Beams: These attach to the posts and form the primary heavy supporting framework around the perimeter of the deck. (On larger decks, beams are placed under the surface of the deck as well, with concrete piers where needed.) Beams are made of 2x6 or 2x8 wood, depending on the distance between the posts. They also bridge any above-the-deck posts, where both posts and beams are usually 4x4s, depending on the design.

Joists: These are heavy wood timbers—usually 2x6s—that run in parallel rows 16 or 24 inches apart between the beams on either side of the deck. The beams are designed to span the long dimension of the deck: joists cross them perpendicularly and are usually supported on top of the beams, close together to support the decking. If joists are fastened to the side of the deck beams, they are bolted through them and further supported by ledgers underneath of the same width as the post.

Decking: This is the surface you walk on.

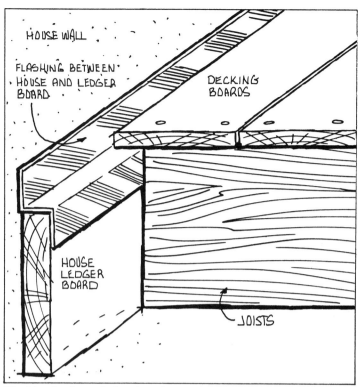

Flashing for house ledger board.

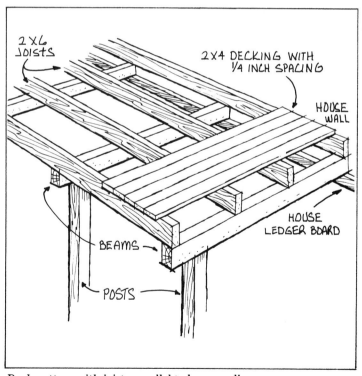

Deck pattern with joists parallel to house wall.

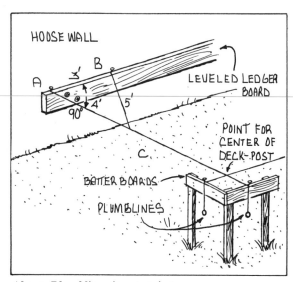

Above: Plumblines for squaring the future deck.

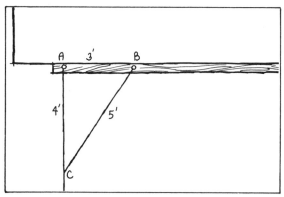

3'-4'-5' ratio to get 90° angle for deck.

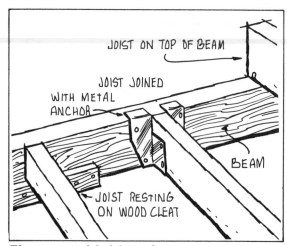

Three ways to join joists to beam.

It's generally 2x4 or 2x6 wood, nailed down flat to the joists and running across or diagonal to them. In the Japanese design, they are nailed with the 2-inch side up.

The Procedure

Let's take these items one at a time and follow through the construction of a typical deck.

Attachment to House: A good many decks are designed so that one edge butts up against the house. In this event it makes good sense to use the house itself as a supporting member. The other advantage of such an arrangement is that there's no possibility of the deck shifting loose from the house so that a gap will form between them.

The first step is to fasten a heavy piece of lumber flat against the house. Use wood of the same width as the joists that support the rest of the deck. (Joists will run from the house to the outer beams.) In other words, if you're using 2x6 beams, the piece that attaches to the house should be 6 inches wide. (See drawing at the bottom of the page.)

The way you fasten the ledger to the house depends on the exterior siding. In the case of stone, concrete block, or the like, masonry anchors will do the trick. Drill through the wood, and temporarily brace it into place against the side of the house. Space the holes no more than 18 inches apart. If the wood is larger than 2x4, alternate the holes, spacing them first toward the top and then toward the bottom of the wood. Mark the position of the holes on the masonry exterior of the house. Drill into the stone or concrete using a carbide-tipped drill, and tap masonry anchors in place. Thread lag-screws through the holes in the wood and into the masonry anchors. Use large washers under the heads of the lags. Tighten them into place with a wrench.

This procedure is a bit simpler with a wood house. Use lag-screws, but space them and the ledger so that the screws tighten into the heavy exterior framing of the house. The most rugged spot is the point where the supports for the interior floors are located. The best place to spot these is to check the architectural plans for the house. If the blueprints are not available, you are fairly safe assuming that the supports are located approximately 6 inches below the top surface of the interior floor.

Translating the measurements from inside to outside is not as difficult as it seems. Merely pick some door or window opening and measure from the top of the sill to the floor on the inside. Duplicate this measurement on the outside, adding 6 inches, and you have the marking point for the upper edge of the ledger board.

There's one other problem you may run into. Occasionally the exterior of the house is so irregular that it is easier to shim out a little with woodblocks. Use small lengths of the same wood that was selected for the ledger board.

Shimming out from the house has one other possible advantage. The joint between the deck and the house can sometimes hold water after a rain or snow. This is an invitation to rot. To avoid this, either apply flashing (as detailed on page 54) or else shim out the deck with short pieces of 2-inch-thick lumber as wide as the ledger board and perhaps a foot long. Due to the additional thickness of the spacer block and the ledger board, you will need longer lag screws for a firm attachment.

Foundation Footings—High and Low: The step-by-step procedure for putting up a low deck or patio is different from the routine for a high deck. However, the procedure, as far as the footings for the posts are concerned, is the same for each.

Use small connected stakes (drawing left, above) and white twine to outline the square footage you have plotted on graph paper. Measure diagonal strings to make certain the structure will be square—at a 90-degree angle to the house. When the diagonals are of equal lengths, you are in business. You can also check the accuracy of the 90-degree angles of the corners of your deck by the well-known 3-4-5 system.

At the left corner, facing the house, measure 3 feet along the house with a string. Project a second string 4 feet out, and from the end measure 5 feet back to the end of the 3-

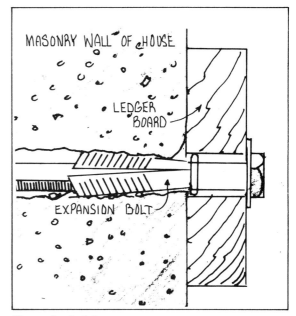

Expansion bolt for masonry.

foot line. This results in a 90-degree angle for your deck (drawing, left middle). Extend the 4-foot string to the stakes where you want your first foundation post to be.

From your graph-paper plan, determine the points on the ground where you will place the supporting posts away from the house, and mark the spots accurately. Depending upon the strength and thickness of the timbers you will be using, (see table on p. 39) upright supports can be spaced 6 or 8 or 10 feet apart. However, check the building regulations in your community first. There may be specific regulations about this.

Dig the holes for the footings. Keep the sides of the hole reasonably straight. If frost and frost-heaving may be a problem, be sure the bottom of the hole is well below the frost depth in your area. (A local plumber can give you this data. Each winter, plumbers thaw enough pipes to have this information at their fingertips.)

Pour concrete into each hole, filling it up within 6 inches of the top. Use packaged concrete for this job. It comes in large paper sacks, and you merely mix the contents with the specified amount of water: you will wind up with a workable mix that will set to proper hardness. Now set the pre-fab concrete plinths into the concrete. Or, if you are pouring concrete posts, after you have filled each hole, poke 2 or 3 reinforcing rods into the wet mix. If they fall over, keep adjusting them until the concrete begins to set; then hold them upright. The rods should be long enough to extend 6 inches above the level of the ground.

When the concrete has set, locate the post-hole that's in the highest ground area. Usually you can spot this by eye. Set a length of pole or scrap wood on top of the concrete, and fasten it to one of the reinforcing rods with string. Calculate how high above the ground you want the finished deck to be by marking the line along the house, leveled with the carpenter's level.

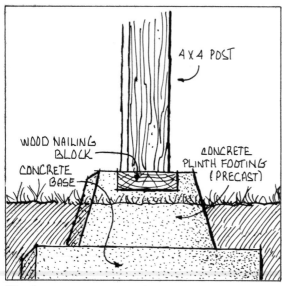

Wooden post on concrete pier.

Deduct the thickness of the decking, joists, and beams. The figure that remains represents the height between the ground and the underside of the deck beams, and this is the height that the posts should be.

Place a board across from the house ledger to the stick above the shortest point. With the carpenter's level, make sure the board is level. Using this as a guide, make a pencil-mark

where the under edge touches the upright stick you've tied to the reinforcing rod. From this point, measure up the stick a distance equal to the deck-height figure you've just calculated. Make a second mark at this level. That will be the top of the deck.

Attach sticks to each of the other footings, tying them to the supporting rods as before. The next step is to extend a level line from the uppermost part of the first stick to each of the other sticks on top of each footing. Here's how it's done:

Tie a piece of stout string (mason's twine is good for this purpose) to the first stick exactly at the upper mark. If necessary, drive a nail into the wood at this point so the string won't slip. Hook a plumbline into the string and stretch it toward the next footing in line. Hold the string so it rests up against the second stick. Jockey the string up and down until the bubble in the carpenter's level comes to rest in the center. Mark the exact spot where the string touches the second piece of wood. Move further down the line and do this with the third footing, then the fourth, and so on.

For the record, what you have done is to extend the mark on the first stick in a perfectly level line to all of the others. This means that your deck will be level *despite any slope or irregularities of the ground.*

Carefully measure the distance between the pencil-mark and the concrete for each footing, and make a note of this exact dimension on your chart. The piers, the concrete sections that fit on top of the footings and underneath the beams, will be of different heights so that they will compensate for the irregularities of the ground. The numbers you have just calculated represent the heights of each of the piers that will go atop each of the footings.

Different Types of Piers: To fabricate piers, you can first make a form for them. There are several ways to do this. Some large building-supply companies sell tubular forms (see page 107) which you can cut to length with a saw. You may instead find it convenient to build an open-ended wooden box. Perhaps a batch of 5-gallon cans with the ends cut off will do. Whatever shape you select, the form should be higher than you need for the height of the pier.

Grease the inside of the form so that the concrete won't adhere, and place it on top of the footing. Measure up the inside of the form and make a mark representing the height to which you want to pour the concrete. Mix a new batch of concrete and carefully add it to the form exactly level with each mark. Before it sets, add the hardware that will attach to the underside of the beams (see page 43).

The procedure is little different if you are building a higher deck. The posts will also have to be adjusted to fit the ledger board against the house and the irregular terrain where the deckposts are to be. After you have poured the concrete for the footings and it has set completely, the prefab piers will be

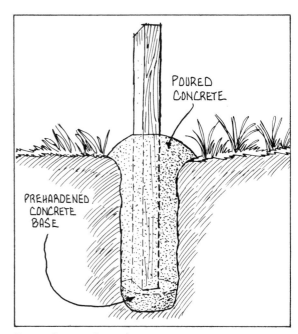

Cementing wood post in ground on hardened concrete base.

fixed on top. With this exception: follow the same procedure with the reinforcing rods that is used on a low deck. The variation depends upon what material you plan to use for the posts.

Wood posts: If you intend to use wood posts (usually 4x4s), fit shorter reinforcing rods into the concrete so they will not extend above the concrete form when it is finished. The same materials can be used to form the piers as described before. Or, if their ends are treated against rot, the posts may be set on the concrete base and concrete poured around them, mounding it above ground.

The next step is to calculate the exact height that the posts should be, so that when they are set on top of the piers, their upper ends will all be level with each other and with the ledger board of the house. Although professional builders use a "transit" for this and for other leveling operations, you can get by with a variation on the same plumbline procedure used for the low deck foundation, using a string plumbline from the house ledger board.

Drive longer stakes into the ground right alongside each pier. Select a pier that is on

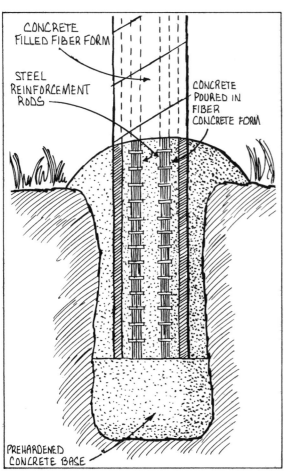

Cementing fiber form post in ground.

the highest ground (visually). Stretch a string plumbline from the ledger board, check the level with the carpenter's level, and make a mark on the stick. Tie a string around it at this point, and drive a nail in at this spot so the string will not slip. The procedure is the same as in the drawing on page 48, but the sticks are higher, to level for a higher deck.

Hang a line level onto string and stretch it to the next stick in line. Jockey the string up and down until the bubble in the level is centered, and then mark the precise spot where the string touches the temporary stick extending above that foundation pier. Move on to the next pier in line, and repeat the procedure. Continue on in this fashion until you have made a level mark on the stick at each pier.

Measure the distance from the top of each foundation pier to the pencil-mark. Deduct the height of the deck board and beams, and

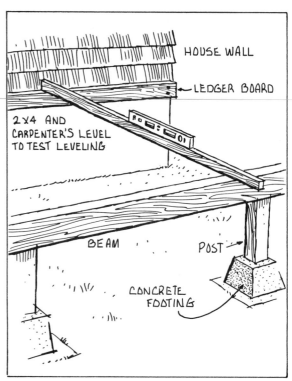

Testing level for joists.

write it down on the graphed outline for each post. Also deduct the distance from the ground level to the top of the first pier. You will wind up with a figure representing the precise length that the post should be on the first pier. To get the height of the second post, repeat the procedure for the lower deck in the drawing on page 48. Use the same procedure for the third one, and for all the rest in the series.

If you are working with wood posts, attach them to the pier and brace them in place with some diagonal lengths of scrap lumber fastened to stakes driven into the ground. (See drawing at left.)

If you are going to form concrete posts, allow the reinforcing rods to extend all the way through the piers and project up above them about a foot. If you are using concrete block for the piers (not aesthetic looking except for high posts), arrange the rods so they will extend through the openings in the block. After you've stacked the blocks on top of the piers, fill the holes with concrete, packing it securely around the reinforcing rods.

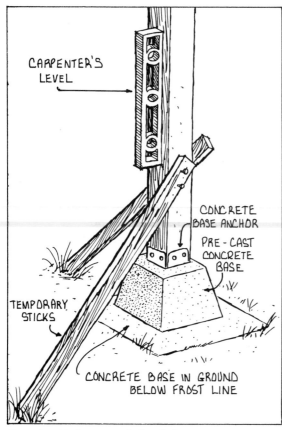

Securing 90-degree angle for deck-post.

It's important that you allow the concrete to harden completely before starting work on the deck above. Concrete sets by a chemical action, not by the evaporation of water. As a matter of fact, it is very important that concrete be kept damp for a period of several days to two weeks so it can develop maximum strength. If you have poured the concrete inside a form, the easiest procedure is simply to leave the form in place, cover the top of the concrete with paper bags or newspaper that you have wet thoroughly, and add a piece of plastic to seal the moisture in place. If this procedure is impossible, wet down the concrete thoroughly with a hose several times a day. Remove forms when the concrete is fully set.

Fit Beams to Post: The next step is to attach the wood beams to the tops of the posts. Using a carpenter's level, make sure the tops of the beams are level with the upper ledger board of the house. If you have to adjust, shim the posts up lightly with pieces of shingle or else cut them off a bit as required. Use preformed metal clips as a connecting joint. These fit on top of the posts and are held in place with long nails (generally 2½ inches long). The other part of the metal clip attaches to the underside of the horizontal beams. The structural purpose of this is to hold the two members together and give protection against lifting of the deck as well.

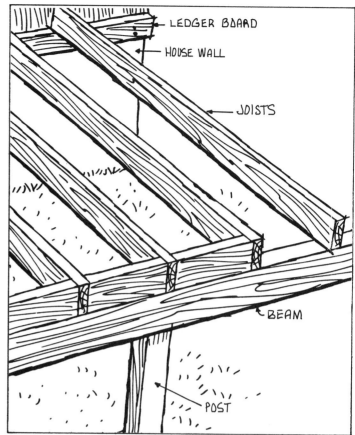

Putting on joists.

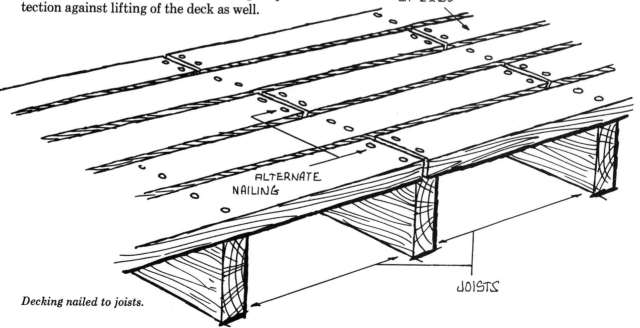

Decking nailed to joists.

Attach Joists: Using metal connectors, fit the joists into place on top of the beams and perpendicular to them; use metal hangers against the ledger board at the other end. As with all other types of metal clips, there's no need to toe-nail. The preformed pieces are face-nailed to the beams, and the joists merely slipped into the saddlelike fitting. Joists are permanently fastened in place with more face-nails through the other surfaces of the hangers. If this method is used, don't forget to nail long lengths of joist lumber to close off the open ends of the beams along the two short sides. These are merely cut to size and spiked to the ends of the beams.

Sometimes metal hangers are used on the sides of the beams instead of the top, but this does not provide as strong a support for the deck surface.

If you are using 2x8 or wider lumber for the joists, it is probably a good idea to provide cross-bracing between them underneath the deck surface. This is the proper time to fit them in place. Use preformed metal bracing for the easiest application. Some types don't even require nails. They have barbed ends that are driven into place on the sides of the joists.

Flashing Prevents Rot: If you'd like to provide additional protection against rot, you can do this by snipping U-shaped aluminum strips with a shears and attaching them to the top of the joists and beams. Flashing aluminum is quite soft. Merely cut the strips to fit over the joist. Position the aluminum so that it overlaps the wood by about an inch on either side. Then, using a small piece of wood as a tool, press down the overlap until it rests flat against the side of the joists or beams and tack them down along the side. This really isn't necessary in most climates where the wood can dry out, but it is wise always to use such flashing with the ledger board along the house (see drawing, page 47). Wherever there is an exposed nailhead in flashing, beam, or roof, you will get leakage and rot unless it is sealed with a dab of roofing tar.

Decking Surface: This next stage is a very encouraging one. For the first time in the course of the construction, you'll begin to get an idea of what the completed deck will be like.

Fasten down the boards that make up the final deck surface. Most common materials are 2x4s or 2x6s. The exact size you select depends upon the dimensions indicated in the table on page 40. Since they also serve as structural members, it's important that the dimensional relationships and spacing of decking joists, beams, and such be preserved.

If you're going to use a water-repellant stain, primer, or paint, it's a good idea to apply the coats to the boards before you nail them down to the joists.

Nailing the Deck: Start putting down the deckboards, beginning at the side next to the house. Use hot-dipped galvanized common ring nails. As the name indicates, these have been heavily coated with a noncorrosive metal so that they'll resist rust. They also have a series of raised ridges spiraling down the shank. The head is large and flat. This handy combination serves the purpose well. The raised ridges hold the nail into the wood with incredible tenacity, as you'll discover the next time you have to pull one out. The large flat head prevents the nail from pulling through the wood in the event of cupping or warping.

In case you are using redwood, cedar, or cypress, you may have some additional expense on your hands as far as the nails are concerned. For these woods, use aluminum or stainless-steel nails. Galvanized nails will stain.

Notice that opposite flat sides of the board are not the same. One of the surfaces is called the bark side, and, if possible, all planks should be positioned with this side facing up. The idea behind this maneuver is to minimize cupping and warping of the boards.

Nail down each deckboard where it contacts each supporting surface underneath. That means nail it down at all joists and beams. For 2x4s, use two nails at each point. Three nails are required for 2x6s and the less preferable 1x6 boards.

Make sure that all end joints between length of deckboards meet over joists, leaving 1/4-inch space between the ends. No end should be flapping loose in the space between joists, or it will sink down every time someone steps on it. Also be careful not to have too many joints between boards falling on any one joist. Visually it is distracting and structurally it is not quite as strong. The end of one board should fall on a different joist than the one next to it. In fact, you can form a sort of pattern of board-ends if you wish.

Don't try to line up the deckboards at either end of the deck. Instead, let them stick out slightly. Then you can merely trim them off following a marked line with a hand electric-saw after you've finished putting down all the boards.

Be especially careful to maintain proper spacing between the boards. For the average deck, the gap between boards should be ⅜ or ½ inch. You'll need space between the ends of the boards too, because they should not butt up snugly against each other when they meet. Three-sixteenths of an inch is a safe amount here. To maintain this exact distance, you will probably find it handy to make a couple of ⅜- or ½-inch spacer boards that you can tuck between the deck lumber as you nail it down. When the deckboards are nailed in place, yank out the spacers and go on to the next plank.

If the deckboards have a tendency to split, there's a trick that old-time professional carpenters use. You might find it handy. They turn the nail upside down and rest the point against a bit of wood, then tap the nail head a bit to flatten the tips slightly. When this type of nail is driven into place, it will partially cut its way through the wood instead of forcing all the wood fibers to the side as is the case with a regular point.

The wood then has less tendency to split. Of course you will still have trouble with the ends of the boards, and flattening the points of the nails won't help here. Instead, use a hand electric-drill to make small pilot holes through the deckboards if necessary. Usually it is not.

When the entire deck is in position, it's time to apply flashing along the house as you have already done with the ledger board (see drawing, p. 47).

Aluminum is the most common kind of flashing used in construction today. Its function, as far as your deck is concerned, is to keep rainwater from seeping down into the crevice between the deck and the house exterior. Cut narrow strips of aluminum (it is very soft, and you can do the job with kitchen shears if necessary). Bend the aluminum into an L-shape. Attach one leg of the L to the side of the house, using a coating of black roofing mastic and small aluminum nails. The other leg of the angle fastens down to the deck with a little more mastic and a few more nails.

However, most people don't like the appearance of the aluminum along the house—even if it's painted. If the deckboard next to the house is nailed down ½ inch away from the house, and if the ledger is covered with flashing, you run no risk of trapping water. When dirt or twigs get behind the first board on top of the house ledger, sweep it out occasionally.

Other Commercial Deck Fittings

If you'd like to make your life a little bit easier, many lumberyards and building-supply companies sell prefabricated kits of hardware that take most of the hard work out of building the structural supports for a deck. Generally, the kits include a series of preformed metal parts, with a lumber list and a set of plans and instructions. Here's a quick run-through on the procedure for building a deck using preformed parts. This particular kit is made by Erecto-Pat, with handsome metal posts and other hardware. Other companies put out similar kits under other brand names.

Stake out the area where the deck will be built. Drive the temporary stakes down into the ground firmly. Tie a string to the stake at a point that will be level with the top of the posts. You can calculate this by stacking up the lumber that will form the deck and measuring it. This dimension will probably be between 13½ and 15½ inches.

Dig postholes at least 8 inches in diameter and about 40 inches deep. The diameter of the hole isn't critical as long as the 8-inch measurement is a minimum. Actual depth of the hole, however, is determined by the frost-line in your area. Position the hole so that the metal posts will be placed approximately 12 inches in from each side of the finished deck.

Fill the holes with cement until the level is 4 or 5 inches below the ground. When the cement has begun to set, push the 1½-inch steel or galvanized pipe into the cement. It should extend about 24 inches into the cement.

Brace the pipe in precise vertical position until the cement has set. The top of the pipe should touch the level line string connecting the stakes. For rustproofing, the galvanized pipe can be painted with a black anticorrosion paint. Slip preformed U-shaped caps that will hold the beams onto the top of the pipe.

Seal off moisture by spreading a polyethylene film across the ground under the area that will be covered by the deck. Punch holes through the film to accommodate the posts. Use 4 millimeter plastic for this job, and cover it with a layer of crushed rock to hold it in position and give a visually pleasing surface underneath the deck.

Stain each piece of lumber before it's used, following the instructions on the container. You'll find it a lot easier to do the job now rather than to wait until the deck is completely up.

Set the beams into the U-shaped fittings on top of the metal pipes. Incidentally, they are known as ground-saddles. The fittings are designed to hold 4x6 beams, although a pair of 2x6s spiked together side-by-side will do quite nicely. Align the beams carefully in the saddles, and then fasten them in place using 1½-inch roofing-nails driven through the pre-drilled holes into the wood.

Nail preformed metal saddles to the tops of the beams. Use 16d box galvanized nails for this job. Space one saddle 12 inches in from each end of a beam. Center the remaining saddles at even distances between these. The exact number you use depends upon the size of the deck and upon the plans that come with the particular kit you purchase. (Complete plans may be obtained from Erecto-Pat at your local lumberyard.) Fit 2x6 joists into

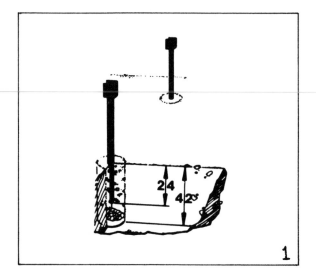

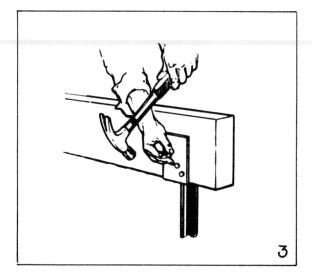

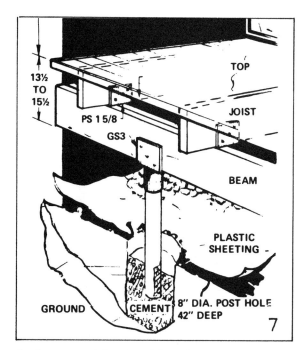

13½ TO 15½

PS 1 5/8

GS3

TOP

JOIST

BEAM

PLASTIC SHEETING

GROUND CEMENT 8" DIA. POST HOLE 42" DEEP

1. Cement upright pipe with preformed anchors in ground.
2. Fit 2x6 beams into anchors.
3. Nail anchors to beams.
4. Nail joist anchors on top of beams, perpendicular to beams.
5. After inserting and nailing joists, lay 2x4 decking and nail to joists with ¼-inch spacing between deckboards, leaving irregular ends.
6. Cut off irregular ends with electric saw.
7. Deck when completed but not trimmed.
8. Nail fascia boards to sides of deckboards to give finished appearance.

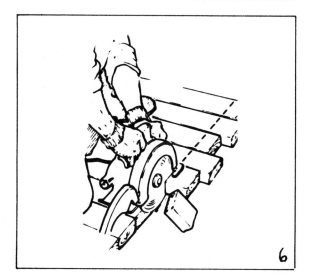

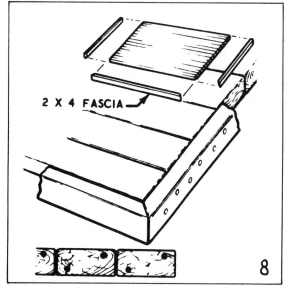

2 X 4 FASCIA

the saddles, align them carefully, and hold them in place with 1½-inch roofing-nails.

It's a good idea to check your local building codes. In some parts of the country they're quite rigid about the spacing of supporting joists. If this is the case, you may have to buy some additional saddles and change the spacing slightly in order to conform.

Form the decking surface out of 2x4s laid flat. Space them the proper distance apart and hold them down to the joists with 16d box galvanized nails. Use 2 nails per joist and try to keep the rows as even as possible for the best appearance.

Don't worry if the deckboards stick out a little bit on either end of the surface. As a matter of fact, don't even try to align them carefully. Instead, when the last deckboard has been fastened down, snap a chalk line against the ends and use a hand electric-saw to make a nice straight cut.

As a final step, add 2x4 trim, called fascia boards, around the edge to finish the deck level with the top of the deckboards. These should be cut to 45-degree angles at the corners and then spiked to the ends of each deckboard around the perimeter of the deck.

Railings

Besides their obvious function of keeping you from falling off the deck, railings also serve a visual purpose. They ease that "hanging in space" feeling that you sometimes get from a deck, especially one that's raised some distance from the ground. And people do feel more secure and comfortable on the deck if it has some kind of barrier around it. The easiest way to incorporate a railing into your deck or patio is simply to extend the supporting posts. As a result, instead of having the floor beams on top of the posts, plan to use thinner lumber for the beams and bolt one timber of the same width on either side of each post. For example, if in your design you are using 4x6 lumber for the beams, on either side of the beams nail 2x6 sections to make the posts. Fasten them in parallel, one on either side of the posts.

Another but similar solution is to make the posts out of laminated lumber. For example, you might use three 2x4s spiked together. If two of them are cut off at the upper end to support the beam while one 2x4 continues upward to form the railing, you'll wind up with an attractive and incredibly sturdy construction. Other suggestions are included in the illustrations on the following pages.

Cut off the post extensions at the proper height all the way around the deck. Use a line level and a string with plumbline to make sure you wind up with an even railing. Use long 2x4 boards that have no warping, and nail them to the top of the posts. Railing-boards join each other (leaving a slight space where the butt ends are nailed in the middle of a post). At the corners of the deck, the railings are mitered, as shown in the drawing at right.

A cap-board railing (a long piece of wood wider than, and nailed flat to, the top of the cut-off posts) is a good idea for two reasons: it will form a firm top surface (the part that people tend to lean on), and it will keep water, which would hasten the unfortunate process of rot, from standing on the top—or end-grain—of the post. If you do not nail a cap-strip in place, do cut the ends of the posts off at an angle so that the water will drain away from the end-grain, or top the post with a square of wood slightly larger.

As for the space between such posts, you can simply nail boards to them at pleasingly spaced intervals or fasten 2x3s spanning the distance between the posts. The fanciest designs have a Chinese arrangement of verticals or squares. A series of rope loops running through small holes drilled in each post can be quite effective and attractive too. As another variation, you might want to cut the posts off at seat level and use them as the back support for a continuous bench that runs around the perimeter of the deck. The seat and the legs of the bench can be made of lumber cut and spiked or bolted to the posts and the deck. For the seat itself, use the same material that you selected for the deck surface or use 2x12s. In the photograph on page 60, you can see the slantbacked railing and seat that is quite popular.

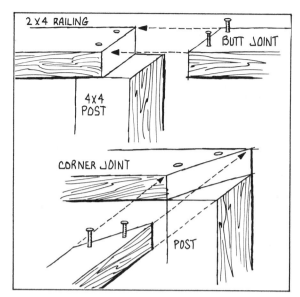

Posts for railings of deck. Above left: parallel upright 2x4s have been nailed to either side of a 2x6 joist and will be spanned and held parallel at the top by the railing. To support the deckboards abutting the upright 2x4s, wooden cleats have been nailed to the uprights under the outer deckboards. Below left: At the corner of the deck, a 4x4 post has been nailed to the end joist on top of the beam, and a wooden cleat nailed to the 4x4 to support the outer deckboard. Above: 2x4 railings are abutted and nailed to the upright. At the corner post, the railings are cut at 45-degree angle and abutted and nailed to the post.

This railing is not a railing at all, but a 48-inch ledge that hides the steep drop below.

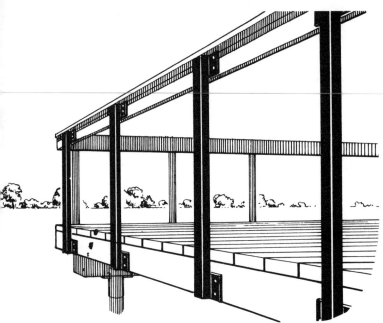

Here, a commercial company has provided square steel railings, with plates at top and bottom to extend from deck joist to railing. The effect is far more handsome than appears in the drawing.

This sturdy bench entirely made of 2x6s has a slant-back bolted to the joists below. With a crossbeam under the seat made of three 6x6s, the front of the seat has 2x4 legs extending through the deck, bolted to joists. Two backrest boards meeting as vertical supports and covered with a cap-board make the bench as firm as possible. Note the V-shaped 6x6 floorboard design, indicating an understructure of beams and joists that is uncommon, making this 3-sided bench possible.

Where a second-story edge of a deck is involved, as in the deck on page 59, a totally different effect may be found. Here a broad rail of no less than six 2x6s protects the high deck, through which the trunk and a large limb of a tree emerge. The wall to the rear provides serene privacy in the direction of neighbors.

If your deck has already been built, or if you prefer to stick to standard construction with the floor beams resting on top of the posts, you can still have sturdy railings without a great deal of extra work. Merely bolt 2x4s or 2x6s to the sides of the outer beams. Use washers under the heads of the bolts and under the nuts to get a firm grip without chewing into the wood. The 2x4s can be fastened either flat or edgewise, depending upon the appearance you want. Space them 4 to 6 feet apart, and fill in between them with ropes, 2x3s, boards, or any other arrangement they will support. The effect will be distinctive.

Some of the companies that make the preformed hardware that simplify deck and patio construction also make similar items intended for fast and easy railing construction. These items consist of steel tubing with flat metal plates welded to either end. The plates are prepunched with the proper-size holes for lag bolts. To assemble the rig, merely bolt the bottom plate to the side of the beams and attach railing materials to the top (drawing page 59). The final effect is quite open, and most people prefer to keep the stark architectural feeling that the material imparts. At right, above, is a variation made by the same company. This is a fine idea, but if there are small children in the household or neighborhood, it may be necessary to install woven bamboo, wire netting, or some firm material to keep them from falling off the deck.

Another possibility involves the use of regular galvanized waterpipe with standard fittings. Cut and thread the material (if you are strong enough) so that the bottom of each pipe fits into a standard socket that you fasten down to the deck with long woodscrews. The upper section should have a pipe T-fitting to support a continuous pipe-railing all the way around the perimeter of the deck. Like the preformed hardware, this variation has that open feeling that many people like, usually painted flat black. (See page 42, where iron pipe is described as a foundation material. And, as stated there, consider buying iron railings instead of fitting iron pipe yourself. Imported railings from the Mediterranean countries are handsome indeed.)

Stairs

Stairs are one of the hardest carpentry jobs that you can tackle. Many professional carpenters dread taking on a job of this nature. Of course, such dire warnings apply chiefly to interior stairs, where the workmanship has to verge on cabinet-making. Calculations in step-making become quite involved. Since all the steps have to be identical, there isn't any leeway to hide sloppy figuring or workmanship. However, before you become too disturbed about this topic, there are several relatively simple ways of solving this common building problem.

First, for an outdoor deck, there's really no need to think in terms of traditional stairs, which have both treads (the part you step on) and risers (the vertical part connecting the treads). Open stairs will do just fine. These are made with nothing but treads nailed or screwed to the stringers, the side-pieces that support the stairs.

For most general utility stairs, a distance of 5 or 6 inches between treads is quite satisfactory. Check the stairs inside your home, and you'll get a better idea of this dimension.

And now for the easiest way out: Many lumberyards and building-supply companies sell preformed stringers. All you do is fasten these in place and add lengths of wood (generally 2x10) to form the treads. The bottom of the stringer must, of course, be anchored in concrete or stone to keep the wood from rotting on the ground.

Slightly more difficult but still not complex is the system of using a pair of 2x10 or 2x12 pieces of wood to form the stringers, with wood cleats nailed or screwed to the inside surfaces as supports for the treads.

Rather than get into complicated calcula-

A variation of the railing fixture on the opposite page is a simple sturdy metal clasp that holds the wooden uprights of the railing firmly to the deck. In this case, you can form a simple railing as shown, or you can vary the pattern of wooden crosspieces and railing in any design that pleases you.

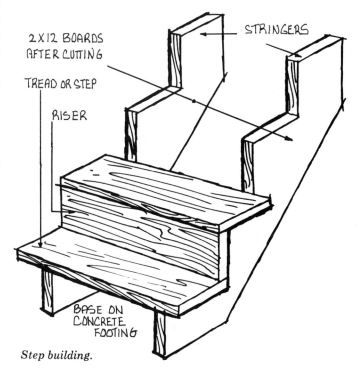

Step building.

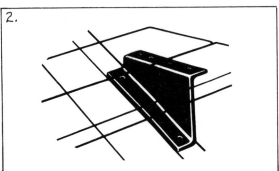

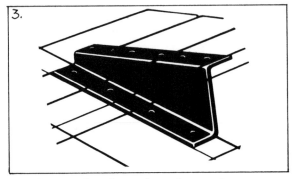

1. When the metal tread-supports have been nailed to the uncut stringers, they give a freer, "floating" appearance than solid steps.

2. A short two-board, metal tread-support.

3. A broader, less steep three-board tread-support.

tions, you can work more or less by the cut-and-try method. Decide on the width of the stairs and place the wood for the stringers in position. Cut off the top end of the boards so they will fit firmly against the vertical beam of the deck. The bottom will fit horizontally against the base support. Then lightly pencil in the position of the wood cleats, using a level. Space them 5 inches apart—top surface to top surface.

When you get to the last step, see how far off you are. If you've been born under the right configuration of planets, the last step may be exactly 5 inches below the top of the deck. If it's anything more or less, raise or lower each step slightly to compensate. In other words, divide the amount of the space left at the top by the number of steps of the stairs. Add this final figure to the distance

between each cleat, and you should be in business. Draw the lines on the inside of the stringers and nail the cleats in place. Cut and fasten the treads to the cleats.

There's another variation of this technique that gives a very pleasing effect out-of-doors. Instead of attaching cleats to the inside of stringers, cut heavy pieces of wood—probably 2x6s—and bolt them to the outside of the stringers. These sections must be long enough to extend beyond the stringer in front and act as a support on which the tread is nailed or screwed. Trim back the outside supports slantwise so they are not so visible and heavy-looking. Cut the treads to a length that will extend out slightly on either side of the stringers and supports.

Simpler to use are metal step brackets (see drawings above). These do not include stringers but are designed to be fastened to stringers in pairs. Most lumberyards and building-supply companies carry these. They are sold together with the necessary fastening bolts.

In some communities, the masonry-supply companies will provide precast concrete steps of various heights to which metal railings can be attached. In such cases, the stair-railings will have to match the deck-railing you use.

Before you get too involved with deciding what type of stairs you want to build, stop and think a moment. Do you really need stairs? For example, will a ramp do as well? For fairly low patios, the answer might very well be yes. Certainly a ramp is easy to build. Undeniably, it's quite handy if you want to roll a barbecue grill onto the surface. Also if there are any small ones around, it can afford much safer access than a set of stairs.

Consider also garden-type steps, made of nontarred railroad-ties or logs.

Deck Wood-finishes

To protect the surface of your wood deck or deck furniture, there are a few words of advice concerning paint that you should heed. You don't have to do it. True, your local paint-store is well stocked with "Deck Paint" and such. You may want to match the color of your deck to your house, with stain or paint, or have a "redwood" color. But you must realize it will wear off in time, from shoeleather and weather. If you must use paint, do so when the wood is completely dry.

But, for longevity and ease of maintenance, paint and stain are not a necessity. If you have built your deck or patio according to the construction details included in this book, it is relatively open. Rainwater falling on it has the opportunity to flow right through the boards into the ground. There should be no spots that will hold and collect moisture.

When it is not exposed to constant moisture, wood is a pretty remarkable material. It can hold up for hundreds of years (literally) without coating or protection of any sort. Most of the horror tales you may have heard about wood-rot have taken place under a specific set of conditions combining moisture, heat, and lack of air. Certainly this trio is deadly, but none of those are present with a properly built deck. Plenty of air will circulate over and under all surfaces. Heat will come and go according to the weather. Ditto for moisture.

The chances are good that your wood deck will hold up perfectly well without any protection whatsoever. If you are insistent upon applying some material, there are coatings designed to increase the longevity of the wood. (For a discussion of copper naphthenate and zinc naphthenate, see page 39.)

Stay away from creosote, except for use on posts or underpinnings that are not going to be seen or touched. This coating has an odor at first, and has a tendency to bleed right through any other coating you put on top. Also on the not-recommended list for the decking are various types of oil coatings. Although they were quite popular many years ago, it was found that they tended to build up on the surface, and sometimes got sticky. Other types discolor as they weather.

If your home is located close to the sea, a brand-new deck or patio can sometimes seem almost raw by comparison with the weathered wood surrounding you. If this is the case, or if you happen to like the appearance of gray weathered wood (as many people do), you can apply a coating that will greatly accelerate the process.

It's known as "bleaching oil," and it comes with various temporary tints built right into it. When you apply this material, the pigment will give the immediate effect of weathered wood. Then it will gradually fade over a period of a year or so. However, during this time, the bleaching agents in the coating will take over and you will very soon have a deck that looks as if it has survived a decade or so in the salt air.

Certain types of stain make an excellent choice for treating the wood, both from a preservative and a coloring standpoint. However, be very careful of the type you buy. So-called penetrating stains do just that. They are light in body and are made so they will sink into the wood. They add tone without hiding the grain of the wood. Heavy body-stains stay more on the surface. They're good for hiding unattractive grain. Whichever type you select, make sure the label definitely states that it is a sealer-type stain. Sometimes the word "nonchalking" is used instead. This means the material will not powder as it weathers and will not rub off on clothes after it has set. If moisture is a problem, stain that contains a mildewcide will keep black fungus-marks from forming on the wood.

For topflight protection while still preserving the attractiveness of natural wood, a combination of a clear-sealer such as zinc naphthenate with a penetrating stain can be highly effective. The good thing about a stain finish is that there's never any need to remove it completely for refinishing—as is the case with paint. Instead, new coatings can just be brushed or swabbed on top when weather exposure causes the tone to fade.

Stay away from the plastic-film type of wood-sealer. This is designed primarily for indoor application. When exposed to extremes of weather, the clear coating tends to chip and peel. When this happens, the only remedy is to strip off the entire coating and start over.

If you absolutely insist upon a skin-type finish and are willing to foot the bill, the new epoxy resins will do the job. Originally intended for use on boats, they have made the transition to home use. This material generally comes as a two-part package that is mixed together just before using. It can be combined with certain coloring agents at the same time, so that you wind up with a tinted or opaque colored coating. For most of these finishes, you will need three coats, and they should be applied one right after the other, with only about a 2-hour waiting period in between.

Three Unattached Deck Forms

Many of the photographs in this book show decks that are not attached to the house, and they are among the most attractive decks around. They range from the floors of Japanese-style teahouses to garden gazebos with beautiful open wooden screens (sometimes with rafters for vines or boxed roofs), and with specimen trees and plantings that are lighted at night. Shown here are three such basic deck floors. Round ones can be constructed in the same fashion as the hexagonal one. (Complete plans available from Western Wood Products Association.)

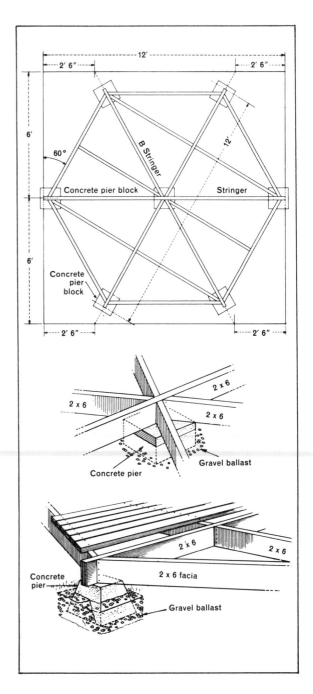

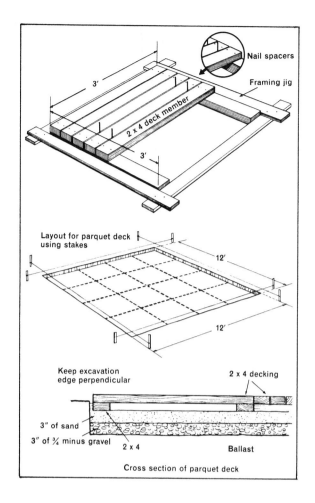

Nail spacers

Framing jig

3'

2 x 4 deck member

3'

Layout for parquet deck using stakes

12'

12'

Keep excavation edge perpendicular

2 x 4 decking

3" of sand

3" of ¾ minus gravel

2 x 4

Ballast

Cross section of parquet deck

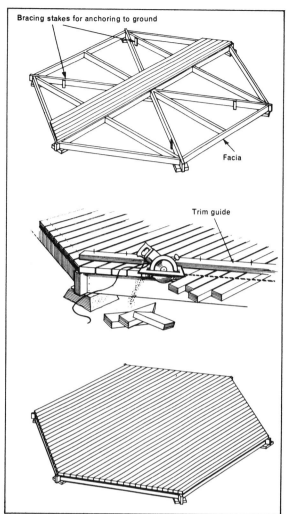

Bracing stakes for anchoring to ground

Facia

Trim guide

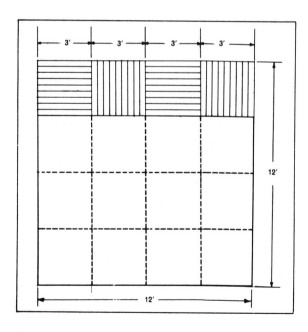

3'   3'   3'   3'

12'

12'

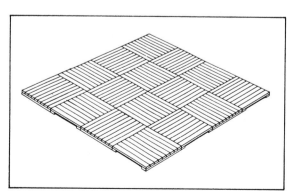

6
Deck and Patio Roofs

Usually, when considering a protective covering for a deck, it's wise to think in terms of a sunshade rather than a major structural roof (which might increase your taxes). Since outdoor-living space will be used principally in warm weather, your main concern will be protecting yourself from excessive sun or a bit of rain. If you're thinking in terms of a full-scale roof, however, it's only one step removed from a complete all-year extension to your house. This is quite definitely a different "ball of wax" from the projects discussed in this book. Be aware that it comes with its own built-in set of headaches.

The load-factor is one. If you live in a part of the country where any appreciable amount of snow is likely to accumulate, it's necessary to provide for this. Snow is heavy, and a foot or more adds up to a staggering load per square-foot. The post-and-beam construction will have to be very substantial. So the major concern of this book involves sturdy but lightweight patio and deck roofs that are intended only to be used as sunshades. They should not be made to support anything more than light coverings that are open enough to let the rain or snow come right through.

Attaching to the House

If your deck or patio directly adjoins the house, the roof-beams can be attached to the homestead one story high. First figure out the height that you want the overhead to be. Start at the outer edge, away from the house. The roof at this point should clear the undersurface of the roof supports by 7 or 8 feet. Because the roof is not designed to support weight of any consequence, you don't have to worry about the pitch or slope of it. As a matter of fact, a horizontal roof may be box-frame or "egg-crate," visually and structurally most appealing.

Start with this flat structural aspect first. Attach the second ledger board one story up, to the side of the house so the top edge of it is on a line with what will be the top of the roof rafters. It's a good idea to apply a strip of flashing to cover the joint where the roof-beams meet the upper ledger of the house. Use aluminum for this, and fasten it in place exactly the same way you

Left: Unusual variation of the egg-crate roof, encircling a southwestern stone house of considerable originality.

This handsome "egg-crate" deck roof has supports over the beams, instead of being flush (the more usual design). Also, it is covered with reeds—with an open strip in the middle—to offer sun as well as shade.

Beyond the bold wall and oriental gate, this solid subtropical roof carries two slender, boxed, open-air vents to light the patio inside. The roof is, so far as possible, hurricane-proof.

did for the joint between the deck ledger and the house (see page 47).

Fasten the 4x4 metal joist anchors onto the house ledger board in the same way that you anchored the 2x6 deck joists to the deck ledger. (See drawing below.)

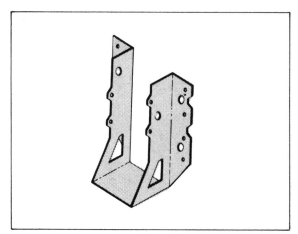

4x4 anchor at house end.

To support the other end (the side away from the house), the 4x4 rafter is supported on the crossbeam in most designs.

However, the 4x4 posts can frequently serve triple duty. They will support the deck, act as railing supports, and hold up the roof rafters at the same time. If the deck has already been completed, or if you can't follow this procedure (not having planned it), you can merely add a second layer of posts on top of the finished deck to support the roof rafters.

Use preformed hardware, such as Teco post anchors, on the top of the deck. (Drawing at the right.) These preformed metal gadgets are bolted to the deck surface. They have a square cup section, into which a standard 4x4 post can be nailed. The final result is quite neat in appearance, and it has the added advantage of raising the post up off the deck surface a bit so that there's no problem with dampness or possible rotting.

Cut the posts to the proper length and stand them in place, fitting the bottom ends into the post anchors. Temporarily add some diagonal bracing made of scrap lumber if necessary (as shown on page 52.) Use a level to make certain the posts are vertical on both sides.

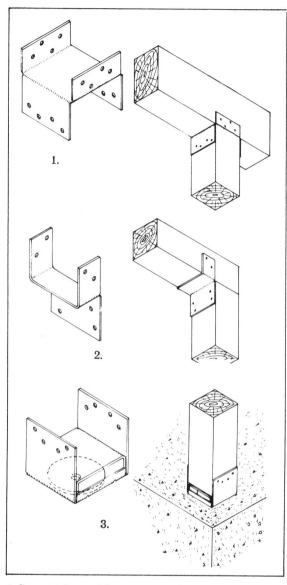

1. Support for roof-beam on top of post.
2. Corner post-cap for roof-beam on top of post.
3. Metal anchor to hold post to surface of deck.

In calculating the lengths of the posts before you cut them, be sure to allow for the beam that will go on top, and also check the space taken up by the post-anchor at the bottom. This is generally $1\frac{5}{16}$ inches, although this dimension may vary according to which type of anchor you purchase. The combina-

A handsome flat deck-roof. Note the 4x4 post on the left (supporting the pressed fiber baffle), the other end supported by the house wall. The beam over the post is a 4x6 supporting 2x6 rafters (the other end of which ties into the house ledger). The roofing is unusual, made up of light 2x2s. The beam, rafters, and roofing all extend beyond their supports.

An architectural roof for a deck swimming pool. Note the rafters extending from the house to the left toward the sun to support the shading overhang. For summer, shade is provided midday by the slatted overhang. The slender 4x4 columns are effectively dignified, the 2x6 deck-plank simple and unostentatious.

Interesting overhang (and roofless) seashore deck-patio. In rough weather, battens are attached to the side against the sea wind. The posts are 4x4s; the beams, 4x6s on end.

tion of post-anchor, post, and beam should be the same height as the distance measured from the top of the deck to the top of the rafter ledger board on the side of the house.

If you want the flat roof rafters to extend out beyond the deck or patio, merely use another foot or so in length for the top 4x4 rafter from the house ledger past the outer beam.

That's for a flat roof. If you want a sloping roof, take the pitch-factor into your calculations. You can figure the pitch on the basis of 2 to 4 inches of rise for every foot of roof. For example, if the distance from the house to the outer edge of the roof is 10 feet, then the back edge (the part connecting with the house) should be 20 to 40 inches higher than the front or outer edge. Calculations of this type have to be very precise if the roof is to hold up under a snow load. Since light covering protection from the sun is the only consideration here, this factor is not at all critical.

At the house ledger, carefully cut and mark the pitch of one 2x4 or 2x6 rafter perfectly. Then use this as a model to mark the other rafters. Place this first rafter in position against the ledger board. If necessary, tack a temporary cleat underneath to hold it in place. You may purchase an angle-iron that will hold the rafter to its supporting beam regardless of the angle (drawing below). Saddle-hangers do not exist premade for all angles of roofs. Look carefully at the drawings,

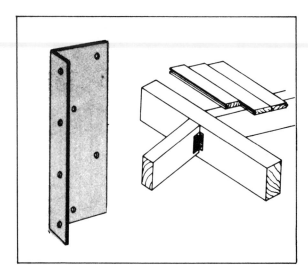

and you'll understand this. Once you have calculated the angle of this first rafter and have trimmed it to a perfect fit against the house ledger, use it as a pattern to mark all of the other rafters for cutting.

At the outer edge of the deck, where the slanting rafter meets the top of the beam, cut the rafter to fit the beam, using a Ty-down metal anchor for a firm joint. Where there is a post, you use one type of anchor (see drawing no. 1, below) to nail the rafter and the post. Between posts, you nail a variation (see drawing no. 2, below) for the rafter and crossbeam.

Cut rafters to the proper lengths, allowing for some aesthetic overhang. For visual effects, and also to shield yourself from the slanting rays of the sun, you may want to extend the roof for some distance beyond the deck or patio. The easiest way to determine this is to tack a broad board to the upper surface of the beam and see just where the shadow area falls in midsummer and extend the overhang to shade the deck.

Roof Coverings

The list of available deck-roof materials is almost endless. It's limited only by what you can find locally, and your own imagination. To start you thinking in the proper direction, there's the old, traditional use of wood slats. These are merely rough 1x2 strips of wood

For a teahouse deck, the solid roof must be of traditional form, though rushes would be more appropriate than asphalt shingles, even in America. Nonetheless, the plastic panels perfectly simulate rice paper, and this house of bonsai protects a priceless collection of the aged trees. 4x4 posts support 4x6 rafters, in turn supporting the 2x4 rafters of the roof.

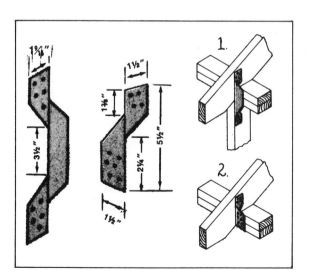

A sunshade roof of 1x2s is supported on 2x6 beams bolted to 4x4 posts. The slanting sunlight casts intriguing optical illusions of an irregular pattern.

A thick reed roof over the Chinese-style screen and strong wood decking of 2x4s set vertically provides the shady part of a sunny pool bordered by pebbled concrete.

lightly tacked to the upper surface of the rafters. Even thinner materials are suitable. You can buy very crude latticework that's just rough-sawn to approximate dimension, but not sanded or smoothed in any way. Stain it before tacking it into place.

A similar material, with the individual slats fastened together with baling-wire, is sold in rolls under the name "snow-fence." Merely dab stain on it, and tack it lightly to the upper surface of the rafters. Less crude, but also effective, is open fencing made of bamboo or cypress slats used as roofing. Basic construction is pretty much the same as snow fence, with lengths of baling-wire holding the sticks or reeds together. It's not necessary to stain this particular material. Just unroll it onto the upper surface of the rafters, and fasten it in place.

For an even finer effect, you may prefer reed. This, too, is available in rolls, generally 15 to 25 feet long. Since the wire used to bind the little sticks together is made of stainless

An atrium patio and lawn, the deck area open to the sky through lattice-roofing, the lawn shaded moderately by stretched plastic screening.

Here the overhead deck provides the roof of subdued light and waterfalls for a garden beneath. Yet lattice is needed for further shading. A unique deck arrangement.

steel, it tends to last a great deal longer than the fencing mentioned above. While you get two or three years' use out of snow-fence or cypress wirebound fencing, reed should last many years longer before the binding material or the wood itself starts to deteriorate. Snow-fence is generally sold in lumberyards, building-supply companies, and sometimes garden-supply houses. The reed rolls are usually only available through nurseries and garden-supply outlets.

Ordinary screening can make a quite delightful surface. It cuts down a bit on the intensity of the sun. For this purpose, use fiberglass screening. Stretch strips of it in place on the roof, and hold them down with staples. This particular surfacing can serve a double purpose. If you should decide to screen in your terrace or patio, you will also obviously have to keep mosquitoes from charging you through the roof. So the easiest way is simply to screen in the overhead. It will not keep mosquitoes, however, from coming up through an open deck floor.

The most rugged and rainproof of the lightweight roofing materials is probably plastic reinforced corrugated panels. As the name indicates, these are formed of heavy-duty plastic in a wavy shape. The problem is that, if you decide to use this material, you must beef up the structural supports of the roof. Since reinforced plastic will not allow the snow to drip through, you're back to worrying about the snow-load factor. Depending upon the section of the country where you live, this could be intense.

Naturally, you will have to have a sloped roof if you use this material. Pitch should probably be at least 4 inches per foot in order to be sure of proper drainage. When you buy the plastic, be sure to pick up some of the preformed wooden, plastic, or cleat fittings made to use with it. The first two come as a series of scallops that match the corrugations in the panels.

Carefully read over the instructions that come with the material. It is essential that you space the joists precisely so they will fall in a direct relationship to the corrugations in the panels. Tack a U-shaped molding on top

The extension of this roof, casting heavy shade from the noonday Florida sun, is a lighter extension of corrugated plastic, letting through the light and air. Over a patio roof, it can serve the same purpose— shielding against the sun without creating a heat-trap.

Seasonal canvas—like the common umbrella—has to be wind-resistant or be folded in a storm. It can serve in many forms over a patio or deck.

Perhaps the most effective of all roofs for a deck is the vine over an arbor facing south or west, where it will shield a house window or a deck. Wisteria and trumpet vines are the most luxuriant. In winter blossoms and leaves are gone, and the slanting rays of the sun reach far into the house or across the deck. Here: Wisteria on an arbor.

of each joist. When you put down the panels, use the special mastic supplied with it (it's usually a thick tape that sticks to the plastic), and overlap the panels as instructed.

To hold the panel in place, drill holes through it into the half-round molding and joists below. Fasten them down with the special nails supplied. These have a wide head with a washer of sealing material underneath.

The scalloped rubberoid or plastic molding is used to seal off the ends of the panels. You will definitely need flashing for this job, and be sure to buy the special material intended just for use with corrugated plastic panels. This stuff goes up with mastic and nails.

One word of caution if you're thinking of using plastic panels to ward off the heat. You may be creating more headaches than you're solving. This kind of material tends to build up heat below; and, unless you provide openings at the upper ends of the roof where the heat can escape, you may very well end up with a hot-box below. Check the instructions that come with the particular corrugated plastic that you select. They will generally have some suggestions for this kind of treatment.

Canvas can be used as a deck or patio covering in many forms: stretched with cord-ties over an open frame, with rafter supports, over and under high and low rafters, or as giant umbrellas.

If the open roof-coverings suggested in this chapter look a little bare and forlorn when you have completed them, don't despair. It will only take a season or two to train a batch of vines to curl over the structure in picturesque fashion.

7
Outdoor Furniture

A scattering of outdoor seat pillows in water-resistant fabric is universal on decks, but you might also give some thought to covering that won't scorch a sitter in shorts or bathing suit. The deck-mattress invites lounging, but it is heavy to carry out of the rain and dew. Another good idea is taken from the wooden lounges of the Austrian *sonnenbad*—the sunbathing spots in the public parks of Vienna. Like our wooden lounge-chairs, they are slatted, but built in a more reclining position, with no cushions. They are easy to construct, and they will lend a sophisticated touch to your deck. Most modern American youth like couches without legs, so a low *sonnenbad* lounge would appeal to them.

For children or for tipsy guests, a broad bench at the deck's edge will serve as protection from going overboard. For little ones, a box covered by a deck hatch can keep rubber balls and collapsed wading-pools out of the way.

The uses of wood are limited only by your imagination. Being so versatile, wood can achieve a hundred uses for the deck, from weathered sculpture to rugged planters. (What better place for plants than on the deck?) Small wooden barrels or jardinieres can hold favorite tender plants, and they can be moved inside when the temperature drops. The seat can be built around a shade-tree, or a large vine can be planted so that it comes up through the deck to cover the deck arbor above. Or wooden boards can be set on edge into the ground to contain a gravel path leading away from the deck steps.

Although the stores are full of patio furniture, ranging from colonial to contemporary in design, many homeowners feel it a shame to wind up a home-designed project with store-bought furniture. There's a great deal of logic on their side. Thanks to a batch of preformed hardware fittings, you can now build sturdy and attractive outdoor furniture in less time than the store takes to deliver. The designs illustrated below show the use of some of these commercial fittings under different brand names. And they look very natural in the photos of deck settings. Most building-supply companies and many lumberyards, as well as the larger hardware dealers, carry this material.

Plain backless benches are easiest to make. Cut 3 lengths of 2x6-inch

*Simple patio bench, with preformed iron fitings, is far more attractive in its natural
setting than a diagram (see drawing on opposite page) would indicate.*

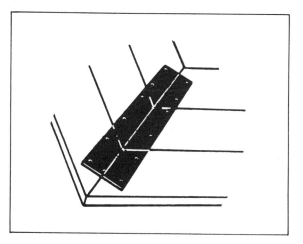

timber. Line them up side by side with a slight gap between the boards, and fasten a pair of the metal supports under them. Space the supports 9 inches in from either end. The brackets can be up to 4½ feet apart and still have maximum strength.

For permanent installation, there's a slightly different bracket that may be preferable. Like the metal post designed to support a patio, these consist of pipe-fittings that are set into concrete-filled holes in the ground. There are also looped legs that permit the benches to be moved about. Depending upon the height selected, these same fittings will produce either a bench or a tabletop. For easy win-

Three-board garden bench on iron legs, the understructure of flat plates screwed into the seat.

The same backless deck benches are formed with U-shaped legs, both as straight benches and as corner benches. These, of course, can be moved at will on the deck or patio, or they can be bolted down.

Swimming-pool garden-seat, with U-shaped prefab legs. Note the Japanese-style seat, with vertical 2x4s screwed into the metal of the legs. Made by the same company that produces the furniture fixtures shown above.

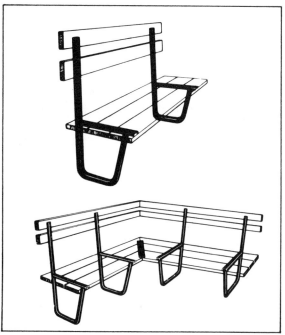

In this northern garden, a 24-inch hexagonal seat around a tree looks out on a unique raised planter or earth fence made of rugged cedar siding driven vertically into the ground.

tertime storage, the entire rig lifts off the pipe supports so that it can be taken indoors, but they can weather the winter as well as any deck if a ¼-inch space is left between the boards.

To build benches with backs, use a pair of brackets that come with predrilled holes. All you do is cut the lumber to length, stain or finish it, and attach the preformed metal pieces. The design shown here uses three 2x6s to form the seat and a couple of 2x4s for the backrest. As a variation on the traditional park-bench design, you can make one in right-angle form. Cut the wood parts to form a 90-degree angle, and hold them together with a bench corner-plate. This design fits beautifully in the corner of a deck or patio and makes a natural conversational grouping.

Many simple or complex garden seats and other furniture may be constructed of boards and nails. Here are two examples—extreme simplicity and sophisticated complexity.

1.

How to build your own all-wood Japanese garden-bench: 1. A 9-foot bench requires three legs, the 7-foot bench only two (see page 82 with firebox). 2. Made of fir or other Western wood, the 9- or 7-foot frame 2 feet wide is nailed together with 16d nails. 3. Vertical 2x4s are placed within the frame, spaced with ¼-inch slats. 4. The 2x4s are nailed into the frame with 16d nails, and the slats removed. 5. The braces are nailed to the bench at a height desirable for comfortable sitting. 6. 2x4 braces cut at 30° angles are drilled and bolted to the 4x4 legs.

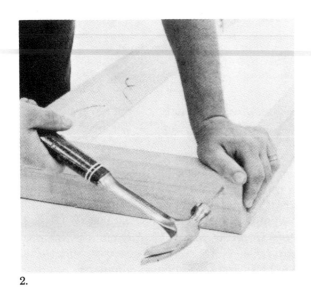

2.

3.

4.

5.

— 6. —

1.

2.

3.

4.

5.

6.

1. Completed garden group, with firebox. Four 9-foot garden seats (see the previous series) are built. 2. Build deck of 9-foot 2x4s laid upright on a 2x4 base embedded in gravel. (Beginning at the firebox in the middle, cut square ends to each board 4 inches longer than the last). 3. Toe-nail upright 2x4 decking to base (sleepers), with each end cut square so no angles need be cut to achieve diamond pattern of deck. 4. Detail of how each square-end deck-board is nailed to the next, in alternating fashion. 5. Completed deck, with firebox in place. Firebox has 5 courses of 4x4x16 concrete blocks bound by mitered 2x6s, attached with carriage bolts. 6. A removable cover is made for the fire-pit to serve as a table when needed; shown bottom-side-up in the photo, it is assembled of 2x2s, with the inside of the smaller frame fitting the outside of the fire-pit. (To send for full instructions, see Sources of Supplies.)

1.

1. Finished planter. 2. Floor of three-foot square planter is made of 2x6 tongue-and-groove wood, nailed blind on 2x2 cleats. 3. Sides of planter are made of one 2x10 and one 2x8. Use a space guider to space the 16-inch 2x2s nailed to the sides. 4. The mitered corners are joined with 8 d nails; and the sides nailed to the floor. 5. To complete, join the corners with 2x2s for a finished look.

2.

4.

3.

5.

8
Variations and Combinations

If you have a deck, patio, or terrace and, for one reason or another, you are dissatisfied with what you have, it may be possible to adapt or alter your existing outdoor space to your needs. If weather or insects prevent your using your outdoor space, you can screen it in so that it can be used. (Since you can't screen-in a deck floor of separated boards, this will be possible only for decks, patios, or terraces that have solid flooring.)

Screening-in Your Outdoor Living Space

Size for size, it's hard to beat the annoyance of a mosquito. If you're looking for tranquil comfort, you might want to spend a little extra time to screen in your terrace, patio, or deck.

Before you do, however, check to see if some of the new insect trap lights will do the job. These are designed to attract the mosquito and then either electrocute it or suck it into a closed container via a small fan.

Do not make the mistake of placing the insect lights on your terrace. Instead, position them 50 to 100 feet away. The idea is to attract the insects away from your terrace, not to it. Yellow bug lights are only mildly effective. Besides, have you ever seen what your nearest and dearest looks like under that pallid illumination? Outside torches may also be worth a try.

If screens turn out to be the only acceptable solution, the job is really not too difficult. Your best bet is to make a series of floor-to-ceiling screen units, using either preformed wooden molding or Reynolds do-it-yourself screen moldings.

The wood variety is available by the foot at your local lumberyard or building-supply company. It's a two-part affair consisting of the structural frame itself and a thinner molding that tacks on top.

The whole process is like making a jumbo picture-frame. Measure the area between posts running from deck surface to underside of roof. Cut the wood molding to size with 45-degree mitered joints. Fasten the parts of the rectangle together.

The trick to stretching the screening taut is to cover two screens at one time. Stretch them out side-by-side, and place woodblocks under the outer edges to make stretching easier.

Many decks and outside gardens need screening, particularly at twilight, when mosquitoes emerge in practically every part of the country, except where infestations have been eradicated. In a permanent screened patio, fine wires are often required to avoid sagging of the roof. In the north, screen roof and siding are usually disassembled because of the snowload. However, screen sides and corrugated plastic roofs are practical in this region.

Slabs of wood had been imaginatively imbedded in mortar, to extend a terrace. Instead of attempting a repeat of the same pattern, the owner continued with very broad planking to form a wood area. The effect, intriguing as it was in the first place, has been simplified and beautified with natural wood.

Use fiberglass screening to cover them. It's reasonably priced, and it's the easiest of all screening to work with. Cut a strip long enough to extend from the outer edge of one frame to the outer edge of the other. Using a staple-gun, fasten the screening to these two edges. Naturally the staples should be driven into the section of the frame designed just for this, where they will be covered by a narrow strip of molding.

At this point, you need the services of two helpers. Remove the blocks from the outer edges of both screen-frames, and press these edges down in firm contact with the floor. This maneuver will stretch the fiberglass screen across both frames until it's drum tight. Hold the frames in this position while you drive in all the rest of the staples around the other three sides of each screen. Slice down through the screening to separate the two screens. Fasten the decorative molding trim around each screen, and then trim off the excess screening that projects beyond them.

The procedure for Reynolds do-it-yourself aluminum screening is different but not at all difficult. You buy this material in strips by the foot. Cut the ends at 45-degree angles, and fit them together to form a frame using pre-formed aluminum angles sold with the material.

This screening is made with a U-shaped channel in it that a plastic spline fits into. Lay the completed frame flat on the ground with the spline channel facing up. Cut a piece of fiberglass screening to the proper size and lay it on top. Hold it lightly in position with some scraps of wood or other small weights. Starting at one corner, apply the spline. Force the spline and screen down into the groove. Work in two directions alternately. That is, push down the spline in a 6-inch section from the corner to one side, then do a 6-inch section from that corner to the other side. Go back to the first section for another 6-inch strip, then back to the second, and so on until the two sides are all attached.

When you have one right angle completely covered, follow the same procedure with the diagonally opposite corner.

To hold the screens in place, merely apply

wood strips to the inside surfaces of the posts, with matching strips on the deck and on the underside of the roof. Slip the completed screen into the opening, and hold it in place with screws or with a second rim of wood strips.

Combining Wood with Other Materials

Often the family with a brick or concrete terrace wanting a larger area, but prevented from obtaining it by landscape problems—such as a steep drop or uneven terrain—can solve the problem by extending what they have with a wooden deck. The combination of brick and wood is attractive and natural, and no land-fill is required. Any number of problems can be solved in this fashion. Or a combination can be planned from the beginning.

A handy homeowner may have to know how to lay a certain amount of brick, including a full understanding of the kind of base sand or gravel that is needed, and how to lay brick on top of the base with mortar, which is a somewhat more difficult process than ordinary bricklaying.

As the following photographs show, there are any number of combinations to tax the ingenuity of the homeowner, whether he calls for the aid of local workmen or not. In fact, if he is sure of what he wants, he must be able to oppose the views of his helpers, or get professional help. In the following pages are a few examples of combining wood with other materials that were obviously successful in the outcome—tile, tile with prefab concrete slabs (round or square), gravel, and crushed stone.

Sometimes brick, flagstone, and concrete have to be installed to complement wood decking. Here is a quick course in what you may find yourself involved in.

Brick

Aside from wood, by far the most popular material for terrace construction is brick. It's

Wood blocks form the warm patio of a garden deck, the outer area formed of white crushed marble, cemented.

If you have inherited a brick terrace and want more space, as this owner did, the answer is to rim the outside of the brick with wood decking, seat, and railing, and then frame a wood deck over a sharp drop in terrain, so that even the fine tree is spared. The table and benches that are standing on the brick are made of decking to complement the addition.

A brick terrace in herringbone pattern, but with white brick fireplace for cooking out, white furniture and planters, and white concrete sculpture on a white cement base. The broad board fence gives a relieving quiet to the unusual objects on the terrace.

easy to understand why, when you realize that it is relatively inexpensive and fairly easy to put down. Also, you can stop the job at almost any point and take it up again later. Try this with concrete and you'll have a mess on your hands, unless you construct sections with wood forms that you leave in place. Then you have something quite handsome.

Base Preparation: It's important to start the job properly. Unless you live in close proximity to the beach, where the soil is half (or more) sand, it's not advisable to put the bricks down on top of the ground, because they will soon become uneven. However, you don't need the crushed-rock base that you would need with concrete.

Mark off the area of the terrace. If it is to be square or rectangular, this doesn't have to be complicated. Four sticks and some white twine will do the trick. To make sure the shape is square, measure both diagonals and adjust the stakes and strings until the two strokes of the X are equal. Otherwise lay out the terrace free-style according to your landscape, and give the terrace an edging.

Dig out the earth and grass to a depth equal to the height of the paving material plus a couple of inches. Try to keep the base of the excavation as even and level as you possibly can.

Drainage: If the soil is very wet, if it is in an area of bad drainage, this is the time to put down new drainage lines. Get composition drainpipe at the local building-supply company or lumberyard. Dig 1 or 2 trenches the depth of the pipe diameter plus 8 inches. Make the trenches about 1 foot wide. Line the bottom with 4 inches of crushed rock.

Put down lengths of interlocked, perforated drainage-tile on top of the crushed rock. The sections of the pipe slip together to form a continuous length. Use unperforated lengths of pipe to run the tile away from the terrace. Fill the trenches with more crushed rock, level with the surface of the ground, and then cover with 2-foot-wide strips of tarpaper.

If there is a problem getting rid of the water that will be picked up by the drainage line, direct the pipes into a dry well. This is nothing more than a buried barrel or drum,

perforated at the bottom, with a foot or so of crushed rock underneath it. Water feeds into this container and then slowly seeps into the ground.

To fend off future trouble, saturate the terrace with a strong mixture of any commercial weed-killer. Take precaution that tree or shrub roots are not damaged.

Laying the Brick: Spread a layer of 2 or 2½ inches of sand over the entire excavation. Any kind of sand will do for this—the cheapest that's available is often known as builder's sand. Use a 4-foot length of board as a jumbo rake to smooth the sand into an even, fairly flat layer.

If you haven't already done so, now is the time to decide upon the pattern that you want the brick surface to form. There are many possible variations. Running bond is the most common, and it looks like a brick wall that's been laid down on its side. Joints between bricks are staggered in alternate rows to make an even and attractive pattern. A parquet design is also popular. (This is also known as basket-weave.) There's one other pattern that many homeowners like, called herringbone. It gives a bit of visual movement without ever seeming too busy.

Your supplier will probably furnish you with a brochure of designs. If not, you might try laying some of the bricks out on the ground in various patterns to see which appeals to you. There's one other variation you may want to try. If the bricks are laid on edge rather than flat, you wind up with a narrow, rectangular form. Visually this can be quite effective, but it's obviously more costly, just as it is with wood arranged in that fashion.

Figuring out how many bricks you need for a terrace does not have to be a mathematical hassle. Instead, merely mark off a square-foot of space on the ground and lay the bricks down to cover the space in the pattern you have selected. Count up the number of bricks, multiply by the number of square-feet in the terrace, and add about 5 percent for a safety factor. As for the edge- or soldier-course, merely figure out how many bricks are required to make up a linear foot and multiply by the perimeter of the terrace. Again add the 5 percent safety factor. Total the two quantities and go shopping for the handsomest brick you can find.

First put down the edge-course of bricks around the perimeter of the terrace. As these are laid on end, they go deeper than the other bricks, which are laid flat, so you'll have to dig out around the edge to accommodate them. Carefully align the bricks as you go, adding a bit more sand underneath them, digging out a little earth, or tamping the brick down into position. Use the handle of the trowel for this job.

When the edge-course is in place, fill in the central part of the terrace. Use a small, pointed mason's trowel to smooth the sand and to dig out or add to the layer underneath each brick. As the surface is spread, continually check with a long (4-foot) board to make sure all of the bricks are the same level. Merely sweep the board across the surface. You'll discover the high bricks by feel. Put your eye close to the ground and site under the board to spot the low ones.

Use a piece of $3/8$- or $1/2$-inch wood as a space gauge when you put down the bricks. This will keep them aligned an equal distance from each other.

You will undoubtedly have to cut some bricks into smaller segments to fill in the edges of the pattern. The job isn't hard, but there's a little knack to it. If you're going to do much work with brick, it may pay to buy a wide mason's chisel. If not, a regular cold chisel will do almost as well. Score the brick on both top and bottom surfaces at the point where you want it to cleave. Then place the brick on a flat pile of sand or on the ground. Align the blade with one score-mark, and strike the chisel smartly with a heavy hammer.

The brick will break. The cut should be along the marked line, but don't look for absolute perfection. If need be, you can hack away small additional pieces of brick with the hammer and chisel. If the fracture line is too far off, start again with a fresh, new brick. If the cut edges are rough, you can smooth them by rubbing them together, or by rubbing them with the side of another brick.

With a shovel, fling a thin layer of sand across the terrace. Then, with an ordinary broom, sweep the sand back and forth until it works down into the spaces between the bricks. Sweep any excess off the surface of the terrace. Wet down the bricks and the sand with a fine spray of water from the garden hose. This will compact the layer of sand so that it will be below the surface of the bricks. Allow the bricks to dry, and then follow the sand and broom routine once more. You may have to go through the same procedure once or twice more after the terrace is in actual use.

There's one other technique that you might find useful if you are determined to have a terrace made of bricks set in concrete. When you have finished the terrace, instead of sweeping sand between the crevices of the bricks, use a packaged mortar mix. This comes in a heavy-duty paper bag and is sold by lumberyards and building-supply companies. As before, fling a few shovelfuls of this across the surface of the bricks and then sweep it back and forth to work it into the crevices.

This time when you wet down the surface, use a very, very fine spray on the garden hose, totally saturating the concrete mix. Really soak it.

Wait until the surface of the bricks has dried, and then add more mortar mix, using the same broom technique. Again soak the stuff thoroughly.

For the gentlest wetting-down technique, which won't blast the cement or sand out from between the bricks, set the garden hose on fine mist and direct it upward. Let the water settle back down onto the bricks like a gentle rain.

Keep the terrace moist or damp for two or three days so that the mortar between the bricks will set hard. If this is too much trouble, cover the terrace with a sheet of plastic film after you have thoroughly saturated the bricks and mortar mixture.

There are a few tips that can make the job easier. For one thing, don't be too concerned if you trample or dislodge the sand bed when you put down the bricks. Merely add a bit more sand and rake the surface level as you go, using the edge of a long board.

Flagstone, Tile, and Other Surfaces

Other paving materials can be put down on a sand base in much the same way as brick. Virtually all of them are more expensive, including slate, flagstone, concrete patio blocks, tiles, wood blocks, and cut stone blocks. See what's available at your local building-supply company. Some of the more exotic items may have to be ordered directly from a company that specializes in masonry items or paving supplies.

There are other possible surfaces available, depending upon your ability to scrounge materials. For example, old weathered railroad ties can make a handsome surface. When a railroad is abandoning a line, they will quite frequently tear up the tracks but never bother

A slate or flagstone terrace can be a garden in itself. Between slabs, some covered with lichen, are crevice plants of great beauty—sempervivum, sedum, and arabis. Usually thyme is grown in northern terraces.

to remove the ties. They will almost always give you permission to come and take the ties away free of charge. However, ask permission first. Almost all lumberyards sell them these days.

Embedding bricks or other paving materials in a bed of concrete is an optional technique. However, as far as the average home-handyman is concerned, it is a brutally hard job, and the chances for error are vastly greater.

Poured concrete can make an excellent terrace surface too. Certainly, for durability it's hard to beat. On the other hand, construction requires a much deeper excavation to accommodate a thick layer of crushed rock, and there is the added work of constructing forms and of troweling and smoothing the concrete slab. Unless you are experienced in the handling of concrete, a project like this is not advisable. If you make a mistake in laying down a brick-and-sand terrace, you'll only have the annoyance of pulling up some of the bricks. Make the same kind of error on a concrete terrace, and it will take a pneumatic hammer to get you back to where you started.

Expensive tile often has to be used sparingly, but the design can still be effective. Use squares of cement block, and intersperse with tile, as in this patio, and it is suitable for any garden style.

These large panels of concrete, laid in wooden frames, would be far easier for the amateur to tackle than a larger concrete surface would be. But such work should be done by an experienced mason.

The roof here casts mystifying shadows; the top frame is typical egg-crate, overlaid with 2x2s.

At the edge of a concrete patio, to keep gravel from scattering on the concrete or the grass, 2x4 wood frames are covered with close-mesh hardware cloth.

Appendix: Deck-building Tools

If your present tool-kit consists of a handful of mismatched hand implements in the top left-hand drawer of a kitchen cabinet, you've got to make a further investment before building your deck. While the average complement of dime store hand-tools will, after a fashion, serve an assortment of household fix-it jobs, they are no match for a full-scale construction project. So sort them over carefully. Select those that are sufficiently well-made to speed a day's work.

In some instances, it is absolutely necessary to have both the hand-tool and the electric tool; for instance, the saw. In other instances, though the electric tool may be faster and far easier to work with, it may be more simple to pick up the hand-tool that's right there in a small tool-kit.

Though the tool box may not be a tool, it is impossible to overestimate the usefulness of one that you can fasten shut and carry easily by its handle. It should take in everything from hammer to drill sets.

Another non-tool that it is unthinkable to be without is a carpenter's apron, with pockets to hold different size nails, a hammer, screwdriver, and pliers.

For deciding on replacements or for evaluating the tools you already have, here's a checklist of the tools you'll need, the signs of quality, and a brief primer on how to use them.

Hammer

There are two main types of hammers. The distinction is the type of claw. Best known is the curved-claw hammer. Besides handling the job of driving nails, it can be used to pull them out and to pry apart two pieces of wood that have been nailed together. The other type is called a ripping, or straight-claw, hammer. Professional carpenters usually prefer these for dismantling jobs because the straight claw is better suited for the task of prying things apart.

Curved-claw hammers come in several different weights, but you will probably find a 16-ounce version the best for all-around work. The lighter 13-ounce size, although easier to heft, isn't really suitable for heavy-duty work. By the same token, the 20-ounce variety can be tiring to handle over a normal workday; and, unless you're driving heavy spikes, the extra weight is generally wasted. Ripping hammers, however, usually are heavier. Here the 20- or even 28-ounce head is more common, but the deciding factor should be how much weight you can comfortably swing during a normal working period.

Signs of Quality: Shy away from cast-iron heads. They may be acceptable for driving in carpet-tacks, but don't expect a cast-iron hammer to stand up under any kind of real use. As a matter of fact, it will be quite disconcerting when the head shatters on impact and pieces fly across the yard. Either type of hammer, the curved-claw or ripping, should have a head made out of drop-forged steel. There is also a new technique called rim-tempering that makes the face, or hammering surface, of the hammer less susceptible to chipping. It's an added nicety but not absolutely required.

The handle should be firmly attached to the head. For many years, the only type of hammer available had a wood handle, but this has changed. Well-established on the market are fiberglass handles, as well as steel handles. Both of these have rubber grips to lessen the transmitted shock impact. They are less tiring and more effective to use because a greater amount of the force you exert goes directly into driving the nail. If you wish to purchase one of these, get one that is made by a company whose name you recognize, and buy it from a store that you know and where you are known.

Be sure to accommodate your own personal comfort. Hold and heft the hammer. It should feel comfortable in your hand. Drive a nail with it. The action should be smooth—as if it were a continuation of your shoulder, arm, and hand. Well-made hammers have a certain ability to absorb shock or chatter.

In the event you are addicted to second-hand tools (don't laugh—there are some home craftsmen who really prefer them), don't be alarmed if you come upon a hammer whose striking surface is very slightly dimpled. This means that the steel has a touch of softness to it, which reduces any tendency for the head to skitter across the end of the nail.

How to Use It: Hold the hammer toward the end of the handle as if you were shaking hands with it. Your fingers should wrap firmly around the handle, with your thumb completing the grip. Do not, under any circumstances, utilize that effete technique of extending the forefinger along the handle toward the head. You'll get an aching hand with pain that can radiate up as far as your elbow the next day. Also, don't make the common mistake of "choking" the hammer—gripping it too close to the head instead of toward the end of the handle. The whole idea of the hammer handle is to give additional leverage. The tool is designed for balance; the weight of the hammerhead and the length of the handle should make things easy for you. Advantages are scientifically built in.

A great many home-handymen make the common mistake of keeping their eyes on the head of the hammer as it arcs back and forth. There's no shorter road to bent nails and battered wood. Instead, keep your eye on the head of the nail. For light-duty work, use the force of your wrist and forearm. Heavier blows will take wrist and full-arm action. For jumbo spikes, put all the moxie you can muster from hand, arm, and shoulder into the blow. No matter what type of nail you're driving or how much force you're using, one factor does remain the same: make certain that the face or striking surface of the hammer is perpendicular to the nail at the point of impact; if the face meets the head of the nail at a slight angle, it will bend the nail.

Generally, when a nail bends, the best solution is to pull it out and start over with a new nail. Occasionally you may be able to get by with straightening the nail and driving it home the rest of the way, but the percentages are decidedly against you. As for starting a nail, the standard technique works fine: hold it upright with your fingers while you tap it lightly until it can stand by itself. Then take your hand away and drive the nail home.

When working with common nails (these have large, round, flat heads), the accepted technique is to drive them down so the top of the head is flush with the surface of the wood. With practice, you can do this without denting the wood.

Nail Set

Finishing nails require a slightly different treatment. In this case, drive them in place until the small head of the nail is raised just slightly above the surface. Then use a nail set to drive the nail slightly below the surface of the wood. When you fill in the depression with wood filler and put paint or finish on top, the nails and nail holes will be invisible. For exterior purposes, if you wish, almost any nail can be driven in with a nail set and covered with plastic wood, especially on exterior wood walls.

The nail set, just as the name implies, is a simple tool that's used to drive finishing nails down below the surface. They come in different sizes ranging from $\frac{1}{32}$ to $\frac{5}{32}$ inch. The lip or business end should be slightly smaller than the nail-head you're going to set, although this doesn't have to be as accurate a match as most other aspects of woodworking. Most carpenters can get by with just one nail set. If you've got a choice at your hardware store, select a set with a square handle. This keeps it from rolling away when you put it down.

Crosscut Saw

Generally there are two types of hand-saws that you will need for your new outdoor project, even though you use an electrical saw for most of the hard work. A hand-saw made for crosscutting has teeth that are specially designed to cut across or perpendicular to the direction of the grain of the wood. There are two main elements to consider in picking out this type of saw. One is the length of it, and the other is the point-size or number of teeth to the inch. The more teeth there are, the finer will be the cut and the smoother the newly cut surfaces. However, you will pay a price for this in time. Fine-tooth saws take longer to slice through the same amount of wood. Although the number of points to the inch will range from 7 to 12, most of your work will probably be done with a 7- or 8-point size.

As for length, most carpenters prefer a blade that's about 2 feet long or slightly better. This gives you a chance to take a full stroke with the tool.

Signs of Quality: Price and brand-names are your best general guides. Well-made saws have cutting surfaces that are very sharp and precision-ground to exact shape. In addition to this, the teeth are set—that is, they are slightly bent alternately to one side and the other. The purpose is to cut a saw kerf, or channel, that is slightly wider than the saw blade itself. In this way, the bulk of the saw, the flat metal, won't stick or bind in the saw kerf. Good-quality saws have a carefully and evenly adjusted set to the teeth. That means that the cutting action will be smooth and regular throughout the entire length of the blade. When you cut with a sharp, well-set saw, the work goes smoothly without catching or binding at any point along the blade. Cheap saws do not give this ease of workmanship. Instead they bind and chatter. This is definitely a place where poor tools exact their price.

Pay attention to the handle and how the saw blade attaches to it. Either wood or heavy-duty plastic handles are acceptable. The blade should fasten to it in three places for maximum rigidity. If the saw has a straight back on it, it can also serve as a straight-edge for marking wood. On the other hand, a great many carpenters prefer a sloping-back saw that has a curve instead of a straight line. They claim it has less tendency to stick in the saw kerf.

In the store, hold the saw in your hand. You should be able to grip the handle comfortably. Sight down the back of the blade to make sure it's completely straight. Check the saw-teeth closely. Look for signs of precision filing and a very even set to the teeth. Have the saw resharpened at the hardware store when it begins to feel dull.

How to Use It: Make sure the work is firmly supported. If the end of the board is flapping because you are not sawing straight, it will chatter as you saw, making the job much harder. Use the back portion of the blade close to the handle to start a cut. Pull backward on the blade a few times until you've made a small groove or kerf in the wood. Enlarge the groove with a few short strokes, and then go into complete action, utilizing the full length of the blade.

Save your strength by letting the tool do most of the work. It's designed for this job. There's no need to bear down on the blade. Let it cut its way through the wood. Crosscut saws are designed to cut on the push or forward stroke and to do less work on the pull or return stroke. For this reason, it's more important to keep up a steady pace, using the full length of the blade, than it is to apply any downward pressure. Saw at a 45-degree angle to the surface of the work during the entire job. A steeper or shallower angle will be hard on your arm.

There's one additional tip that may prove useful. Occasionally you'll come upon wood that just seems to grip the sides of the saw no matter what you do. As a result, the blade binds and tends to buckle. When this happens, spray the sides of the blade with a silicone spray (the kind made to ease sticking bureau drawers) and keep working. The extra lubrication will usually solve the problem. In the event you don't have silicone spray on hand, rub the sides of the blade with soap. The result won't be quite as good, but it will probably work well enough.

Always support the loose end of the board that you are cutting. Never allow it to break loose of its own weight as you near the end of the cut. And never break it loose yourself by twisting the saw blade. Instead, hold it in place as you finish the cut with a few very light strokes.

Rip Saw

At first glance, a rip saw looks pretty much the same as a crosscut. It's not, and the big difference is in the teeth. They are filed to a different shape and look like little chisels, so the cutting edges chop their way through the wood. As with the crosscut saw, the teeth are set—that is, they're bent to alternate sides of the blade. However, the set is a little wider so that the saw kerf is slightly wider than the slot cut by a crosscut saw. A rip saw is designed to cut down the length of a board; that is, parallel to the grain of the wood.

Rip saws are slightly different from crosscut saws in one other way. The teeth are set slightly closer together at the tip end of the saw. Since most blades have 5½ teeth per inch over most of the span, the section at the tip will have 6½ teeth per inch. This feature comes in handy when you want to start a cut, because you can use the tip portion of the blade to make the job a little easier.

Signs of Quality: Once more, brand-name and price are good indications of quality. Examine the teeth carefully to make certain they are precision-ground to shape and are accurately set. Sight along them to check the set. You'll be able to spot the unevenness of the set, as is sometimes the case with a cheaper saw. The difference is more than aesthetic. You'll have to do more work for the same job, and it will be a lot harder keeping the saw to the line.

Top-quality rip saws are made with a taper-ground blade. This means it is thinner at the back edge (the part away from the teeth), and it is also thinner at the tip of the blade than it is at the butt end back toward the handle. Although the cost may be higher, such a saw is well worth the expense, because it reduces the amount of effort you have to expend in making a cut. Such a blade will have much less tendency to bind in the saw kerf and will instead cut smoothly and easily down the entire length of a board.

How to Use It: Start the cut using the tip portion of the blade. Form a small groove by pulling backward several times in short pulling strokes. Then, using this groove to guide the blade, start cutting, using short strokes with the tip of the blade first, gradually extending until you are sawing with the complete length of the blade. Once more, let the tool do most of the work. A sharp, properly set saw will slice through wood at a satisfying rate, with only modest pressure exerted on the blade. A rip saw, as opposed to a crosscut, works only on the down or push stroke. Support the work carefully so that it won't chatter as you saw.

When making a long cut down the length

of a board, there may be a tendency for the wood to bind on either side of the saw blade despite the set to the teeth. If this happens, tap a small wooden wedge into the cut at one end of the board. This will hold the two halves apart slightly so that you'll be able to make a free cut.

As with all saws, cut on the waste side of the marked line. Don't try to split the line down the center. That would be inaccurate and virtually impossible. If you find that you get off-course as you're sawing, flex the saw slightly to direct it back to the line as you work. This should be a gradual sort of thing, so that you don't kink or bend the saw.

Keyhole Saw

You might need a keyhole saw, especially if, after building your deck, you need to make a hole for a pipe or to cut around some obstruction such as a slender tree. By drilling a hole with the augur bit, you can get started with your keyhole saw. There's also a power tool for this—the jab saw or saber saw—but you probably won't have enough use for it, so the hand-tool should be a better choice for you.

Screwdrivers

There are two common distinct types of screwdrivers, and you'll need more than one of each. The regular screwdriver that you probably know best has a narrow tip that fits into the screw slot. Although not as familiar, the Phillips screwdriver is becoming more common. It has a star-shaped, pointed tip that is designed to fit exactly into the reverse shape on the head of a screw. The main advantages of a Phillips are that it cannot slip out of the slot and there are more surfaces available for applying the force in turning the screw. The main disadvantage is that the fit of the screwdriver has to be carefully matched to the head of the screw.

Buy a screwdriver of a medium size and length to start. Purchase additional screwdrivers when you buy the screws used for various projects. You will finally wind up with a varied assortment capable of tackling almost any job. Incidentally, screwdrivers are designated by the length of the blade and the width of the tip. This means that an 8-inch screwdriver has a blade that's 8 inches long. Unless you really need them to work in restricted space, stay away from the very stubby screwdrivers. For some reason (it apparently has virtually nothing to do with the laws of science), a longer screwdriver is easier to turn. For the same illogical reason, it's also easier to apply both turning and downward force to a longer blade. When you buy larger size screwdrivers (with heavier blades for larger screws), be sure to get the type made with a square shank rather than a round one.

Signs of Quality: Top-quality screwdrivers have blades made of drop-forged steel. The tips are precision-ground to shape, not stamped. In order to fit firmly in the screw slot without slipping out, the flat surfaces of the blade should be relatively parallel to each other down toward the tip, and should gradually thicken to form the shaft running to the handle. Don't be afraid of plastic handles. Top-quality tools use these nowadays. The important thing is to make certain the blade is firmly and permanently attached to the handle. The only exception might be in the case of screwdriver sets with a series of interchangeable blades that fit into a single handle. With this, you can have the necessary different sizes of both standard blades and Phillips.

How to Use It: The most important factor is to match the blade to the work. Too small a screwdriver blade used to turn a large screw will be damaged. As a matter of fact, you will probably chew up both the screwdriver tip and the slot of the screw. On the other hand, too large a screwdriver tip will not fit into the bottom of the slot and so will have a tendency to pop out as you turn. Even if you do manage to turn the screw all the way down, the overhang of the blade on either side will chew up the wood during the last few turns.

In almost all cases, you should make a starting hole for the screw. For small screws, a small hole pressed into the wood with a gimlet will probably do the trick. A gimlet or awl is nothing more than a metal point attached to a handle. Gently tap a finishing nail to make the hole, if you don't want to bother with a gimlet. Gently turn the first few threads of the screw into place. Hold the screwdriver perpendicular to the surface. Turn with one hand as you guide the tip of the screwdriver with the other, until at least ¼ of the screw is into the wood. Then you can concentrate on driving it home.

When driving large screws, you can get some additional leverage by hooking a wrench onto the shank of the screwdriver. (That's why you were advised to make sure your largest screwdrivers had square shanks.) Another tip is merely to coat the threads of the screw with soap before starting it. The soap will cling to the metal and act as a lubricant as the threads bite into the wood. Also, for larger holes, it is very important that you drill pilot holes, usually with your hand drill, for both the threaded section of the screw and the unthreaded shank of the screw. (The electric drill has a special attachment for this, if you want perfection.)

Folding Rule

The most commonly used measuring tool is probably a 6-foot folding rule. Buy a good one with clear, accurate markings and metal joints that snap into open and closed position with a reassuring firmness. Examine the markings on the rule carefully before you walk out of the store. There are many types made for special purposes that will be confusing in general use. For example, some rules are made with the markings designated in feet and the markings for inches are indicated only up to the first 12. But the standard rule has the inches in sequence as the principal markings, and the feet designation is secondary.

Measuring Tape

For large-scale work, such as the projects you will be tackling, you'll also need a long measuring tape. A 50-footer is not that much more expensive than the 25-foot variety, and

you'll probably use it a great deal more. Again, make sure that the markings are clear and legible and that the device has a hand-crank handle for winding the tape back into the case. The spring-type that self-winds is only available in the form of shorter tapes.

Combination Square

Two types of squares should complete the list of necessary measuring tools used to mark lumber for sawing at various-degree angles. The first is a combination square. For slanting railings or decks that are not square or oblong, you will need it. It has a handle and blade that can be assembled in different configurations to mark and measure 90- or 45-degree angles. For cuts of less than 45 degrees, you will need a protractor square. Some of the more expensive squares include a bubble-tube so you can use the device for leveling and a pointed marker tucked into the handle for scratching marks into the work surface.

Plumbline

As shown in some of the illustrations of this book, it would be impossible to build a deck without a plumbline. This is a long cord, with each end tied through the eye of a plumb-bob, a lead weight. When the cord is stretched over the top of posts or across beams, it is possible to determine whether they are level by hanging a line level (see below) on it, or by holding a carpenter's level under it. When the posts are aligned, and a beam placed temporarily across them, you can then use the carpenter's level to doublecheck the height.

Line Level

You should also invest in a line level. This inexpensive gadget is only a few inches long and is quite lightweight. It has hooks or clips at each end so that it will hang on a plumbline or taut string. You'll find it quite handy for work in grading or leveling the tops of beams and posts (see page 52).

Carpenter's Level

Invest in a carpenter's level in a 2-foot or 4-foot length; make sure that it has bubble-tubes in both horizontal and vertical positions. The more elaborate varieties also include a 45-degree tube, but this is not really necessary for most work. The body of the level can be either wood or metal; just make sure that the basic construction appears sturdy.

Carpenter's Square

You will certainly need a carpenter's or rafter square. This large metal device is actually two metal rulers joined at right angles, specially made for measuring and marking the 90-degree square on 2x4 studs, rafters, stairs, and such. Buy one with clear, well-etched markings in $\frac{1}{16}$ inches on it for easy reading, and it should be at least 3 feet long horizontally and 2 feet vertically.

How to Use It: Strangely, a person who has never used a square before finds it difficult to mark a 90-degree angle across a board because he does not consciously realize that the long end of the square must fit perfectly to the side of the board so that the short end will make a perfect angle for marking. The result is a marking that can be sawed square. It seems too trivial to mention, but nonetheless necessary to point out to an amateur who is working alone.

Pliers and Wrenches

You will need a pair of slipjoint pliers, which lock in two positions. Those made of top-quality metal usually say so somewhere on the tool itself, with the words "drop-forged steel" etched or stamped into the metal. Channel or pump pliers are made so the jaws can be locked into several different positions to accommodate different thicknesses.

The combination plier-wrench is much less common; most people have never seen one, but it can be quite useful. This gadget has an adjusting knob that sets the jaws to the precise distance apart that you want. It might be confused with the adjustable wrench, which also adjusts in width but doesn't have the gripping-wrench teeth, and has only one handle. When you squeeze the two handles of the plier-wrench, the jaws will lock closed until you release them.

The adjustable wrench is the old reliable tool mentioned above for turning nuts or square-headed bolts. Although more expensive, socket wrenches are quite a bit faster to use if you have a lot of bolts of one size to tighten, such as those that bolt heavy beams to posts or to an entire deck. Just as the name implies, these have a series of metal tubes or sockets, each one designed to fit one specific type of nut or bolt. All the sockets snap into an offset ratchet handle. By simply swinging the handle back and forth, you can turn the fastener with great speed. Because of the leverage of the handle, the last few turns used to tighten can have quite a bit of power behind them. If you are bolting beams, use a socket wrench as well as an electric drill to get the bolts in. Don't depend on 9- or 10-penny nails to hold your deck up forever if the beams are fixed to the side of the post instead of on top.

Brace-and-Bit

Even though you may have an electric drill (see below), you'll still find use for a brace-and-bit. Be sure to get the ratchet type so that you can swing the handle back and forth to turn the bits in tight space. At the same time, buy a set of auger-point bits in standard sizes to fit the brace. You can get adjustable ones that will drill up to a 3-inch hole through wood.

Woodplane

A woodplane in a size called a jack-plane is probably the handiest smoothing tool you'll have in your kit. The base or bed of this plane is usually 12 to 15 inches long and takes a blade that's 2 inches wide. Teamed up with a carefully sharpened and honed blade, a plane is a delightful tool to use as it trims neat spirals of shavings off a board.

Chisels

You will probably need an assortment of chisels. There are two main types. A firmer chisel is made with a thick blade and is intended for heavy-duty work. You can drive this one with a mallet (if it has a wood head) or a hammer (if the metal tang of the chisel blade extends all the way through to the back end of the handle). Paring chisels are much thinner and are intended for hand-use only. Don't bang on these or force them because you can snap the brittle metal. Work with a light hand to make the finishing touches on carefully fitted joints.

Miter Box

If you do not acquire an electric saw that adjusts for the depth of cut and the angle to be sawed, a miter box will be needed. Usually a special saw, called a backsaw, is used with the box, but it is possible to work with a standard crosscut saw.

Ripping Bar

If you are an amateur, you'll need this "goosenecked" crowbar with a slit for pulling heavy nails. It is popularly known as a "nail puller." Try to get a 4-inch nail out of a 4x6 plank with a claw hammer, and you'll soon learn why. This bar will pull nails because it is 18 to 30 inches long, and no nail made can hold out against the leverage that it provides. The other end of a ripping bar has a chisel that can loosen anything from an imbedded nailhead to a stubborn floorboard that has been crookedly nailed to a joist.

All-purpose Snips

Surely you will have to snip aluminum or copper flashing and also wire at some time or other, especially if you decide to use the inexpensive wire fencing to fit the deck-railing.

Sandpaper

Every time you saw a board, you have to smooth the edge. You would be surprised how some amateurs and even professionals think it doesn't matter, but a moment's effort in removing raw edges may be the chief difference between ragged-looking and handsome woodwork. You don't need an electric sander for this. And many a child's fingers or adult's clothing may be saved from splinters or tearing.

Saw-horse and Woodworker's Vise

At the risk of discouraging the deck-builder, one of the most satisfying big carpentry jobs an amateur can tackle, it is necessary to mention only two more nonpower devices—a woodworker's vise, which can hold lumber or other material while you work on it, and the saw-horse, across which you can handily control the lumber while sawing. You can use a ladder and a stool, but why not put together two saw-horses with saw-horse brackets, disassemble them later, and use the lumber for something else? It will make the job easier all around.

For All Electrical Tools

Wear rubber, not plastic, gloves while using all electrical tools, no matter what other safety devices the tool, electrical cord, or extension cord may have.

Electric Drill

From the home-handyman's standpoint, the handiest thing to come down the pike this generation is undoubtedly the portable electric drill. Inside this palm-sized powerhouse is enough moxie to drill through the toughest steel, with the precision necessary for fine work.

Drills are categorized by size, and this is determined by the largest drill-shank that the chuck of the tool will accept. In other words, if the biggest drill you can normally get into the tool is ¼ inch, the drill will be known as a ¼-inch electric drill. The same tool comes in ⅜-, ½-, and ¾-inch sizes, but these are mostly the province of professional artisans. The power available to twirl the bit also varies considerably, although the range is somewhere between $\frac{1}{5}$ or $\frac{1}{6}$ of a horsepower all the way up to better than a full horsepower. The tool will be used chiefly for drilling boltholes or masonry. It is possible to avoid both if you have no masonry foundations and if you put your beams on top of your posts. But it will be handy for starting large nail- and screwholes.

Safety Features: Be sure the drill you buy has electrical safety features built into it. This can take the form of a 3-wire cord (two prongs plus a round peg contact on the plug), or the tool can be built with an isolation-type construction that separates you from harm should a short-circuit develop within the mechanism. These drills are generally called "double-insulated," and you should look for these words on the label or instructions.

Don't bypass the 3-wire cord and plug if your drill is equipped with one. Use a 3-wire extension cord, and make sure that the final socket that you plug into is equipped in a similar fashion. Most drills are sold along with an adapter plug that consists of a fitting at one end for the 3 connectors, plus 2 prongs and a loose wire at the other end. Connect this wire to one of the screws on the 2-hole plug electrical outlet. This will ground any short-circuit. Don't neglect this simple step or you will cancel out the important safety precaution that's been engineered into the tool.

Some brands of portable electric drills nowadays come with a variable speed switch. When you pull the trigger, it does more than merely turn the rig on and off. A very gentle pull will set the drill to remove quite slowly. Squeeze the trigger all the way back and you've got full speed. In between is an infinitely variable range.

This simple feature can provide quite a handful of convenience. For example, you can attach different screwdriver bits to the chuck and use the electric drill to drive wood-screws. It's easier on the drill-bit if you use low speed when boring a hole in hard metal. The same applies to making a hole in concrete, brick, or stone. These are just a few of the instances when a variable speed feature can prove to be well worth the additional slight expense.

There are a whole host of accessories available for the drill. The list includes a flexible shaft attachment, right-angle attachment, grinding wheels, grinding discs, circle cutters, hole cutters, hacksaw attachment, rasp, various types of sanders, and even a paint stirrer.

Hand Electric Saw

Like the drill, this tool adds up to a tremendous amount of useful power available to your right arm. The most convenient type of power-saw for home use should be capable of cutting through a piece of 2x4 lumber at a 45-degree angle, as well as 90 degrees and any direction in between. This makes such a special piece of machinery as a miter-box superfluous.

For the most part, it takes a blade that's about 7 inches in diameter. Most saws actually use a blade that is $7\frac{1}{8}$ or $7\frac{1}{4}$ inches to ensure a complete cut. At the store, check over the power-saws and make sure the one you select has a depth adjustment so that you can make shallow as well as deep cuts. You see, circular saws operate best when they are adjusted so that the blade just cuts through the bottom of the work. Make sure the tool also has an angle adjustment, so you can make bevel cuts. A ripping fence is also standard. This guides the saw so that you can zip right down a board maintaining the same width along the entire cut.

Make sure the tool has an automatic spring-loaded blade-guard. This is a semicircular gadget that retracts as you cut into the wood. When you finish the cut, the guard swings around to cover the exposed blade.

Buy the electric saw that feels comfortable and workable in your hands. Make sure the tool has either a 3-wire cord and plug or a double-insulation feature so that you will be protected in case of malfunction. As with an electric drill, the size of the motor and its power varies considerably from one brand to another. Generally, it's directly linked to price. Buy as much tool as your pocket-book will sustain, providing you can still heft and handle the saw with ease. The more powerful saws tend to be larger and heavier.

Jab Saw

If the family budget will stand the expense, two other tools will quickly repay their cost in terms of time and effort-saving. For making curved cuts such as rounding bench corners, a reciprocating or jab saw has few equals. This is made with a sturdy but stubby blade sticking out of one end. Pull the trigger and this blade moves in and out with a rapid reciprocating motion. Teeth on the blade are designed to cut on the up-stroke. If you have this, you don't need a keyhole saw, and vice versa.

Belt Sander

The other tool is a belt sander. Just as the name indicates, this power abrasive device uses an endless belt of sandpaper (generally about 3 inches wide) running over a couple of drums driven by a powerful motor. For smoothing a surface in a minimum amount of time, few tools can match the work output of this one. The belts are available in several different grades or grits of abrasive, so that you can begin with very coarse grit for rapid cutting and gradually shift to the finer grades for a smooth, ready-to-finish surface. Hand sandpapering all the wood of a deck can be very time-consuming.

SCREW CHART

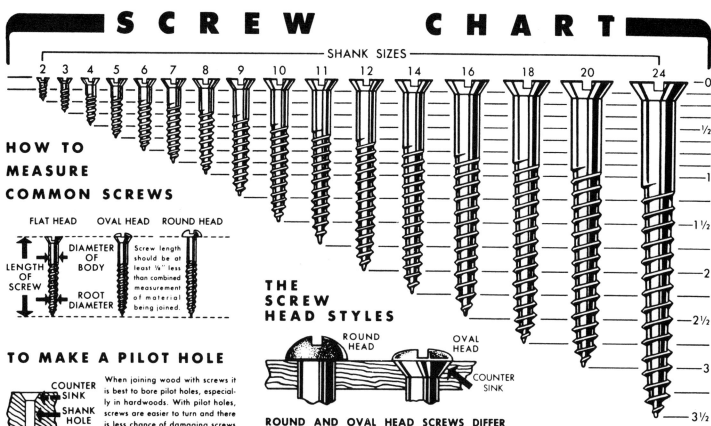

SHANK SIZES

2 3 4 5 6 7 8 9 10 11 12 14 16 18 20 24

— 0
— ½
— 1
— 1½
— 2
— 2½
— 3
— 3½

HOW TO MEASURE COMMON SCREWS

FLAT HEAD — LENGTH OF SCREW, DIAMETER OF BODY, ROOT DIAMETER

OVAL HEAD

ROUND HEAD — Screw length should be at least ⅛" less than combined measurement of material being joined.

TO MAKE A PILOT HOLE

COUNTER SINK — SHANK HOLE — PILOT HOLE

Pilot holes for small screws may be made with a brad awl, a gimlet or ice pick.

When joining wood with screws it is best to bore pilot holes, especially in hardwoods. With pilot holes, screws are easier to turn and there is less chance of damaging screws or wood. Bore holes large enough to easily accommodate screw shank in first piece of wood. Bore holes slightly smaller than thread diameters to a depth of half the length of threaded portion in second piece of wood. In hardwoods use a *fine thread* screw; in soft woods, use a *coarse thread*. Countersink to slightly less than diameters of screw heads.

THE SCREW HEAD STYLES

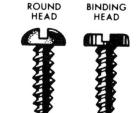

ROUND HEAD — OVAL HEAD — COUNTER SINK

ROUND AND OVAL HEAD SCREWS DIFFER FROM THE FLAT HEAD ONLY IN HEAD STRUCTURE. THE THREAD IS THE SAME. THEY ARE GENERALLY OBTAINABLE IN THE LENGTHS AND GAUGES CHARTED IN THE ABOVE DIAGRAM.

SHEET METAL SCREW STYLES

FLAT HEAD   OVAL HEAD   ROUND HEAD   BINDING HEAD

Two main types of Sheet Metal Screws are produced . . . Type A and Type B. Type A is intended for the joining or fastening of sheet metal 18 gauge or lighter. Type B is for use on sheet metal up to 6 gauge. Both types have the following head styles . . . Flat, Round, Oval, Binding and Stove. They are available in lengths from ⅛" to 2" and in these shank diameters . . . No's. 4, 6, 7, 8, 10, 12, 14. For best results, drilled or punched guide holes should be slightly smaller than screw diameter.

PHILLIPS SCREWS WITH RECESSED HEAD

This screw is best identified by the cross-shaped slot in the head. It is made in nearly as wide a range of sizes and gauges as the standard screw. It requires a special driver. Two sizes of Phillips Drivers fit the Phillips screws most often used.

PHILLIPS SCREW

PHILLIPS SCREW DRIVER

MAKE SCREW DRIVING EASIER   FOLLOW THESE SUGGESTIONS

1 For easier driving, drill pilot holes . . especially in hardwoods.

2 Pick out a screw driver blade that seats snugly in the full width of the slot in the screw head.

3 Use as long a screw driver as possible; this gives greater leverage.

4 Keep driver square and flat in screw slot.

5 Hold driver in line with screw and apply steady, even pressure; hold screw with other hand until it is firmly started in the wood. Once started, most force is used to turn driver.

6 Seat screw firmly and snugly. Too much pressure can strip wood or break screw. (If pressure becomes too great before screw is fully driven, withdraw screw and rebore hole.)

Soaping or waxing threads on large screws makes them easier to drive.

DOWEL PIN

AUGER HOLE

SCREW TOO SHORT

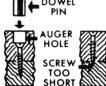

Countersinking by use of auger bits is done to conceal screws with dowel pins or to extend screw deeper and more securely into material being joined.

HOUSEHOLD SCREWS FOR SPECIAL USES

CUP HOOK   SCREW HOOK   "L" SCREW HOOK   SCREW EYE

THESE SCREWS ARE USUALLY AVAILABLE IN SEVERAL SIZES AND METALS

NAIL CHART

The chart below illustrates nails in most common usage. Most are available at your hardware dealer.

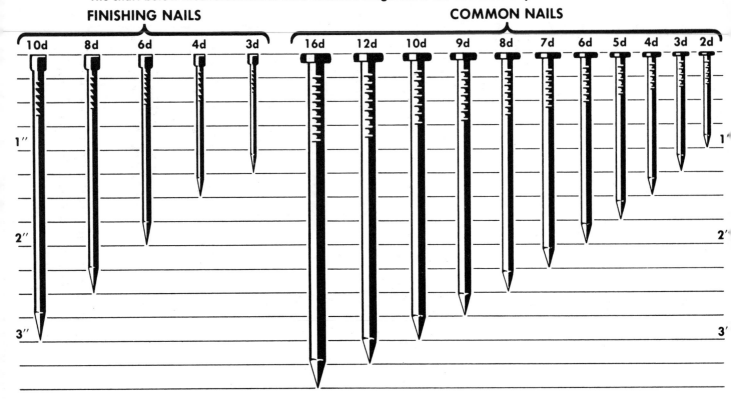

FINISHING NAILS

10d 8d 6d 4d 3d

COMMON NAILS

16d 12d 10d 9d 8d 7d 6d 5d 4d 3d 2d

1″ 2″ 3″

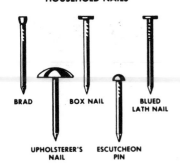

HOUSEHOLD NAILS

BRAD BOX NAIL BLUED LATH NAIL

UPHOLSTERER'S NAIL ESCUTCHEON PIN

HOUSEHOLD TACKS

WIRE UPHOLSTERER'S TACK BILL POSTER TACK UPHOLSTERER'S TACK

DOUBLE POINTED TACK CHECKER HEAD CARPET TACK GIMP TACK

REFERENCE TABLE-COMMON NAILS

Size	Length and Gauge	Diameter Head	Approx. No. To Pound
2d	1 inch . . . . No. 15	11/64	845
3d	1¼ inch . . . . No. 14	13/64	540
4d	1½ inch . . . . No. 12½	1/4	290
5d	1¾ inch . . . . No. 12½	1/4	250
6d	2 inch . . . . No. 11½	17/64	165
7d	2¼ inch . . . . No. 11½	17/64	150
8d	2½ inch . . . . No. 10¼	9/32	100
9d	2¾ inch . . . . No. 10¼	9/32	90
10d	3 inch . . . . No. 9	5/16	65
12d	3¼ inch . . . . No. 9	5/16	60
16d	3½ inch . . . . No. 8	11/32	45

REFERENCE TABLE-FINISHING NAILS

Size	Length and Gauge	Diameter Head Gauge	Approx. No. To Pound
3d	1¼ inch . . . . No. 15½	12½	880
4d	1½ inch . . . . No. 15	12	630
6d	2 inch . . . . No. 13	10	290
8d	2½ inch . . . . No. 12½	9½	195
10d	3 inch . . . . No. 11½	8½	125

OPEN OR FACE NAILING

is used where there's plenty of room to work. The nail is usually driven into the work at a right angle or nearly right angle to the surface. As illustrated above.

CLINCH NAILING

is used to fasten boards face to face. Nail should be about ½″ longer than thickness of two boards. Bend projecting nail ends towards each other. See above.

TOE NAILING

is used in joining vertical and horizontal boards. Drive nails from both sides well into the wood before driving either one all the way in. See the above diagram.

Sources of Supplies

Teco
5530 Wisconsin Avenue
Washington, D.C. 20015

Western Wood Products Association
1500 Yeon Building
Portland, Oregon 97204

California Redwood Association
617 Montgomery Street
San Francisco, California 94111

Lloyd Lumber Co.
2 Allview Avenue
Brewster, New York 10509

Erecto-Pat Inc.
32295 Stephenson
Madison Heights, Michigan 48071

Index